MW00526211

How They Prayed

Vol. 1—Household Prayers

How They Prayed

Vol. 3—Household Prayers

By Edwin & Lillian Harvey

UNITED STATES ADDRESS
Harvey Christian Publishers, Inc.
449 Hackett Pike, Richmond, KY 40475
Tel./Fax (423) 768-2297
E-mail: books@harveycp.com
http://www.harveycp.com

BRITISH ADDRESS
Harvey Christian Publishers UK
11 Chapel Lane, Kingsley Holt
Stoke-on-Trent, ST10 2BG
Tel./Fax (01538) 756391
E-mail: jjcook@mac.com

Printed in USA
First Edition 1987
This Edition 2014

ISBN: 978-1-932774-76-4

Cover Design by
Isaac Samuel
faithgrafikdesigns@gmail.com

Printed by
Lightning Source
La Vergne, TN 37086

Foreword

The title of this book was suggested by a series of articles which my husband and I wrote for the periodical, *The Message of Victory,* which we edited for forty years. Since my husband's death, I have enlarged the articles and have added more material from our files from other sources dealing with the same subject. *How They Prayed,* Volume 1, includes how husbands prayed for their wives, wives for their husbands, children for their parents, and parents for their children. It also cites examples of grandparents whose prayers prevailed for their posterity.

Prayers are deathless. Those members of a household who have praying relatives are of all individuals most fortunate. This book has been written with a deep, heartfelt prayer that the contents might stir others to pray that the home might be preserved in its purity and power as an influence upon the nation and world.

I am deeply indebted to my daughter, Trudy Tait, to Edward Cook, and to Beulah Freeman who have given invaluable time in order to make this book possible. Much prayer has been made during its production for blessing on the readers.

Lillian Harvey

June, 1987

Acknowledgments

In seeking to obtain permission for copyright material used in this book, we have met with a most courteous and gracious response from both Publisher and Authors. We take this occasion to express our thanks in the following instances:

To Nicola Brook Michel for permission to use extracts from her book, *Teenage Market.*

To the Faith Mission, Edinburgh, for permission to use an article from *Bright Words* on Annie Bowie.

To the Faith Mission, Edinburgh jointly with The African Evangelistic Band, Cape Town, for permission to use material on the life of Harriet Garrett.

To the Herald of Holiness of Nazarene Publishing House, Kansas City, for permission to use portions of the article on Biblical Illiteracy and for the article, "Prayer Changes Me," by Katherine Bevis.

Many of the poems, quotations, or extracts have been accumulated over a long period of years from various sources. We have been unable to trace the Publishers or Authors in some instances, and if we have used any material which should have been acknowledged, we beg your indulgence, and we will make proper acknowledgment in future editions of this book.

Contents

Home—the target of the enemy. . . .

How We Need Home Intercessors

"The breakup of the family is not incidental, but central to official Communist ideology. This was one of the ideas on which Lenin insisted most strongly," said Elton and Pauline Trueblood. And the breakup of the home is tragically upon us. When "living together" has become acceptable, and our young people are openly defying the God-given directives as to marriage and home, we need desperately to plead with Christians to pray earnestly that prayer may take its proper place in the homes of today.

Christians whose homes used to resound with the sound of hymn-singing and prayer before the day began, now start the day with a rush and a hurry, as Mother, too, must get ready to abandon home for the workshop, office, or factory. Mothers used to place a high estimation upon the honored role of motherhood and homemaking. There she could quietly and in an orderly fashion direct the affairs of her dominion, grasping order out of chaos. There, too, she reigned as queen, making home a beautiful place for children and husband to return to at night. One can tell by the look on a child's face whether or not they have a mother who cares enough for them to sacrifice higher standards of living in order to be at home with her family.

Now the children sometimes are left to get off to school without Mother to wave them off. They arrive home from school to find the home empty, and no longer does the familiar call, "Mother," bring response from the keeper at home as she welcomes her loved ones to the majesty of "Home." Mothers have exchanged the exalted task of child-rearing for making more money to buy more things to clutter up the home. Garage sales and basement sales are the outlet to sell off unwanted goods which the extra money has purchased. How threadbare our values have become!

Mothers used to take time to pray! Mothers used to take time to visit the elderly, the widows, the fatherless, and many times supply them with a welcome hot bowl of soup, or an oven dish which they had ample time to make when preparing for their own family. Now roadside cafes have taken over the catering for "motherless" families who need a good breakfast before the day's work.

Mothers used to be the intercessors for their loved ones still outside Christ. Women used to intercede for the local church, for the missionaries out on the field. Women used to intercede for the evils which were threatening the wellbeing of their own sons and daughters. Women used to be the ones who offered hospitality to the traveling evangelist or a soul in need. Is it any wonder that Satan has aimed his arrow right at the home—the bull's eye on the dartboard of the universe? Oh, if we could only alert noble-minded women to go to prayer and refuse to be a part of this Satan-inspired conspiracy to downgrade our Christian countries, thus influencing their daughters and other young women as to the exalted privilege of holding the character and purity of the manhood and womanhood in their hands.

And what about the tired, jaded husband confronting the world all day at office, or farm, or the factory, or in public office? Does he come home to be able to confide in the noble partner of his choice the struggles he has made with the flaunting immodesty all about him? Or does he find a wife likewise contaminated by the same kind of peer pressure from the world all about her, too weary to contend with the heartbreaks and confidings of her husband? Little wonder that adultery resulting in divorce is increasing in our Christian world.

What about the lack of employment? If women would revolt and stay at home instead of vying with men-folk for jobs and careers for which they were never created, the plight of our Western world could be solved without political parties using unemployment as a propaganda issue. Unbelievers, through breaking down Bible standards, have fostered this imbalance, hoping to upset the Christian standards which in the past have brought such blessing to our land.

We must commend those women who defy fashion and custom and stay at home, refusing to leave their little ones to uncaring adults who have no religious convictions. Their homes are like beacon-lights in the darkness of our night; their children, the hope of maintaining our Christian heritage!

To prayer! To prayer! There links in the chain that hold our civilization together, and we have been made to feel that materialism is the hope of the home, the neighborhood, the country. While polishing up that materialistic link, we have neglected the Bible and prayer, and tragedy is not far away! We are on the verge of going the same way other civilizations have gone in the past who worshiped the golden calf and rejected God.

Some years ago the Queen of England broadcast a message to the women of the British Empire. Among other excellent things she said was this: "It does indeed seem to me that, if the years to come are to see some real spiritual recovery, the women of our nation must be deeply concerned with religion, and our homes the very place it should start. It is the creative and dynamic power of Christianity which can help us to carry the moral responsibilities which history is placing on our shoulders. If our homes can be truly Christian, then the influence of that spirit will assuredly spread through all the aspects of our common life, industrial, social, and political."

"We hear much about revival today, but it is always in connection with the church," said O. Dale Emery. "I wonder if perhaps God is saying to us, 'You're working in the wrong place.' Ask God to bring revival in your home. If He does, I'll guarantee it will infect the church. And I believe it begins when you and I establish a value system—a priority system—to meet the needs every day with our families."

We close with a poem by Grace Crowell.

So long as there are homes to which men turn,
  At close of day;
So long as there are homes where children are,
  Where women stay—
If love and loyalty and faith be found
  Across those sills—
A stricken nation can recover from
  Its gravest ills.

So long as there are homes where fires burn,
  And there is bread;
So long as there are homes where lamps are lit,
  And prayers are said—
Although people falter through the dark,
  And nations grope—
With God Himself back of these homes,
  We have sure hope.

Busy Marthas. . . .

How They Didn't Pray!

"There are five hundred Marthas for every Mary, and so I fear the Christlike character is much wanted in many of us. . . . Remember from whence thou art fallen," said an English evangelist. Busy Marthas are highly esteemed by our materialistic society with its unbiblical standards. Marys are considered outdated and old-fashioned. But Christ highly commended Mary, saying, "Mary hath chosen the better part which shall not be taken away from her."

The things which outlast time have been sacrificed for the temporary luxury of having everything. Parents have allowed the world to squeeze them into its mold by sheer peer pressure. Women have become slaves to the high standards of western living, making bricks without straw, overworking to pay for the trivial, while paying dearly for preoccupation with "work" and losing our most valuable investment—our children.

In the media we hear that authorities are troubled over the high incidence of teenage suicides, and they cannot understand why this should occur in our affluent society. The reason seems most apparent to us. Adults have woefully neglected their own flesh and blood, failing to take the time with them, failing to pray for their well-being as they enter a world where everything beckons them on to destruction.

Some few years ago while in Britain, a youth club leader handed us a book, shockingly frank, entitled, *The Teenage Marketplace*. It was written by two teenagers who decided to frankly commit to paper their verdict on our modern, western culture. There is much in the book that we would prefer to be more delicately written, but it is an indictment upon home and society.

One of the youthful authors was from a wealthy British home. It was a fashionable custom to place the child in a boarding school at an early age. The author graphically portrays her emotions as she wistfully watched her parents' beautiful car disappear down the drive, and she was left alone to face a completely new life in strange surroundings. Not once did her parents give one backward look or one final wave to the insecure youngster whom they had brought into the world and for whom they were responsible.

She also remembered another wistful time when thoughts of death were confusing her young mind. She so wanted someone adult to explain it to her, and she had gone outside on their estate to think about it all. Her father discovered her out in the grounds in the twilight, but his only concern was that she might catch cold. What might have been the story had her father cared enough to try to understand the mental torture this young daughter of his was undergoing, or realize how dreadfully she was requiring an explanation of the mysteries of life!

At boarding school, this same youngster discovered one of her teachers to whom she might have confided her perplexities, but she bemoaned the fact that "she was over busy, too busy." So on through those difficult early teen years went this adventurer in life, without the protecting care of parents or teachers. We have often visited elderly people in old people's homes, and the repetitive complaint is that their loved ones so infrequently visit them. We reap what we sow!

Let us ponder what this English teenager says in her indictment of our adult world: "I was mad with my parents when they lectured about having certain standards to live up to. I couldn't understand what standards. Was it the standards of randy Lords in the government who slunk off secretly to lay prostitutes and took drugs? Or the Watergate bugging standards? Or were they talking about the standards I read about all the time in the press and saw on television—violence, pornography, cheating?

"Perhaps it was the standards of a fashionable boarding school with frustrating stripteases in the dormitory, yobs queueing in the lane, little Pakistanis and others with their dope, filthy books, and magazines for girls that treated sex like a new invention?

"Or was it the standards of knowing how to lay on a perfect cocktail party, the right apologies, the right amount of snobbery, the false sweetness of a voice on the telephone, the sickening hypocrisy; knowing how to arrive late to show that you were not drooling to come, had visited bigger mansions, more important people; the right tone of voice when you said how pleased you were to see someone you despised? I was desperate, felt cornered—was there only this artificial life and the other one of perverts in Piccadilly, grunting hippies, pot-smoking?

"One Sunday morning my mother called me a heathen because I hadn't gone to church with the family. She said it laughingly, but it hurt. I still couldn't find myself paying homage to a God Who was brought out for an hour once a week in a sermon.

"Deep down inside of me I was really yearning for someone I loved and respected to explain to me decisively what it all meant, what I ought to do. I know I was not the only one. How I wish now that my parents had got hold of me, even forbidden me to leave the house on some of my stupid outings—discussed it, helping, explaining!

"But why couldn't I see for myself that I was being exploited, how the pop, porn, sexy journals, TV, and films, were killing my girlhood and artificially rousing my awakening sexual desires. Why can't girls see through it before they become doped or ruined? I suppose an awful lot of the adult world don't want to see through while they're cashing in. I'd just like to hit back at those who would injure me while virtually a child without caring, only for profit, and these people were all adults.

"We teenagers of all classes are reached and degraded by exploiters through discotheques, TV, pop festivals, magazines, etc. In fact I've noticed that there are probably more of the so-called privileged ones caught up in the exploiter's net. Could it be that the privileged have a less well-knit family life, due to boarding schools, materialism, superficial society, where no sort of adversity holds us together as a family? It is noticeable how the privileged teenagers of today search for primitive and basic things.

— 13 —

"Men have no morals, and we can't depend on them." (Had she never met a truly godly man?) "The guardians of a nation's morals, and that means masculine strength, are ourselves—women. We are the losers in the end. When we give way a nation falls apart—the hand that rocks the cradle rules the world. A burnt-out woman is finished; a burnt-out man can find a woman to pull him round. What the grown-up world does behind closed doors is their business, but can they give us a chance by not dragging us into it? We loathe those adults who debauch and degrade our young bodies for profit, and those who shrug apathetically when we mention it."

We digress in the above in order to convince mothers and fathers that their first obligation is to God and their God-given home responsibilities with their children. We heard the other day of a young couple who between them—husband and wife—were holding down four jobs. What about their children?

Time! Time! Time! The stuff life is made up of, and we are spending it like the prodigal in riotous living, making money to purchase those things which we shall have to leave one day, and neglecting those eternal interests which in the next world shall find us paupers and spendthrifts.

"For one, I care little for the government which presides at Washington," said the Rev. Theodore Cuyler, "in comparison with the government which rules the millions of American homes. No administration can seriously harm us if our home life is pure, frugal, and godly. No statesmanship or legislation can save us, if once our homes become the abode of ignorance or the nestling place of profligacy.

"The home rules the nation. If the home is demoralized, it will ruin it. The real seed corn whence our Republic sprang was the Christian households represented in the *Mayflower*, or the family altar of the Hollander and the Huguenot.

"All our best characters, best legislation, best institutions, and best church life were cradled in those early homes. They were the taproot of the Republic, and of the American churches."

Appalling ignorance of modern youth. . . .

How They Didn't Read Their Bibles

How many young men and women have told us of how they never had one adult ever approach them seriously, even in the church, to discuss the problems of evils to which they are exposed daily. Even in those churches that teach a deeper life, material gain has become the preoccupation, and while we have been so busy here and there the young folks have gone, feeling deprived of the mature counsel and companionship of adults.

The Bible admonishes parents to teach their children the Bible: "And these words, which I command thee this day, shall be in thine heart: And thou shalt teach them diligently unto thy children, and shalt talk of them when thou sittest in thine house, and when thou walkest by the way, and when thou liest down, and when thou risest up" (Deut. 6:6, 7). That kind of training seems all too prosaic and boring a matter because it demands too great expenditure of time. The modern tempo of life will not allow us to teach them rising up, for there is one mad rush to get off to work; because mothers are away from home, they cannot obey the command to teach when they sit in their house. The family scarcely ever takes a walk together, so "as thou walkest by the way" is out. As to when you lie down, that also is too demanding, for after the toll on our energy we are just too plain tired to obey this very overt command.

Judges 2:10 tells of a condition which exists in the Western world today: "And there arose another generation after them, which knew not the Lord, nor yet the works which he had done." This was because after Joshua died and all the elders that outlived him, someone failed the young people, for they knew not God nor the mighty deeds which He had done. We in the Western world are in the same plight, as will be seen in an article which appeared in *Herald of Holiness* in 1966, written by Richard Lyon Morgan, professor of Bible at Peace College. Doubtless the situation is even more deplorable after the lapse of over twenty years.

"It does not take long to realize the glaring ignorance of the content and message of the Bible among believers today. Nowhere is this ignorance more evident than on the college campus. Despite the fact that many students are products of the church, and that, in the case of Christian colleges, many more are products of Christian homes and have been exposed to Sunday schools for many years, their knowledge and understanding of the Bible is little better than that of millions of people who make no Christian profession. They may be nominal followers of Christianity, but they have never really heard the message of the Bible, nor do they know the simplest facts of the faith.

"A student once said, 'If a Communist were to ask me what I believed about the Bible and the Christian faith, I wouldn't know what to say. I've gone to Sunday school and church all my life, but they just haven't given me a living memory of anything.'

"Evidence of this Biblical illiteracy is seen in the results of a test given to 150 freshmen in a church college. Practically all these students were members of a Christian church and had never known a day without religious influences. The test in no sense indicated how a student would interpret the Bible, but dealt only with elementary questions about the Bible, such as: Where was Jesus born? Which was the earliest of the four Gospels? Name some of Paul's letters. Who was the successor to Moses? Name two of the Hebrew judges. Name a Wisdom Book. Where do you find the account of the Lord's Supper? What book tells the history of the Early Church?

"Answers were revealing. The story of Abraham was found in the Book of Ruth. The Roman persecutions were the great event of the Old Testament. The Exodus was the return of the Jews to Palestine after World War II. The Ten Commandments were given by Jesus from the Mount of Olives, and some of the

Wisdom Books of the Old Testament were: Acts, *Paradise Lost,* and *Lord of the Flies.* Jesus was born in Rome; His mother's name was Gabriel, and He was baptized at Pentecost by John the Baptist in the Red Sea. The earliest of the four Gospels was Genesis. Moses turned the Red Sea blue during the Exodus, and Joan of Arc was the Hebrew heroine who saved her people from the hatred of Haman. The mother-in-law of Ruth was Mary Magdalene, and her famous great-grandson was Noah. Jesus was betrayed by Samson and died at Bethlehem.

"The average grade of the test was ten percent, and the highest was 34 percent. Over half the students left three-fourths of the test unanswered. These results in no sense reflect on the intellectual abilities of the students, for all of them had survived the many hurdles that would have kept the unqualified from entering college. But the results do point to the real crisis in the teaching of the Bible in church and home. And this Biblical illiteracy is not restricted to college students.

"Will Herberg has said, 'Though four-fifths of all Americans acknowledge the Bible to be the "revealed Word of God," when asked to name the first four books of the New Testament over half of these same faithful folk could not mention even one.' Despite all the outward signs of religious revival and the tremendous increase of church membership and church buildings, there exists 'a famine . . . of hearing the words of the Lord.'

"The Biblical illiteracy in the church today presents frightening possibilities. The Christian faith is always one generation away from extinction. If the church does not communicate the faith to its young people, there are ominous signs for the future. Elton Trueblood, in *The Company of the Committed,* has said, 'What reason is there to suppose that our civilization, in contrast to other civilizations which have preceded it, will survive? There is no high probability that the fate of our civilization will be different unless. . . .' Unless? Unless we communicate the Biblical faith to our young people and acquaint them with the sacred writings that alone can make them wise unto salvation."

All of this stems back to the personal failure first in our own lives to take time with God and in reading His Holy Book. We take hours before the godless "box" in our home where we view the world's ideals all the time. It is little wonder that we are conditioned to what the prince of this world can present to us as the ideal. The Western nations need repentance to God for the woeful lack of conscience in matters that have to do with home and children—our priceless possessions. Dope pushers take time to peddle dope. Prostitutes take time to entice the young in the streets and public places. Pornographic publishers take time to produce hellish literature with which to sully the minds of our children, but churches spend all their money in erecting costly buildings, and neglect the priority of publishing uplifting books.

Oh, how we plead for praying mothers and fathers who will deny themselves some of the modern extras in order to make time for converse with God and meditation on the highest subjects that affect the eternal destiny of themselves and of their children!

Praying mothers have been the finest recruiting officers for the pulpit and mission field the church has ever had. We do not have the same quality and calibre in the ministry today, despite the fact that educational advantages are plentiful. Is it mere chance that this is so? What mother, emerging from a prayer session with the Eternal God, could engage at meal time in frivolous talk about salaries, fame, and assured futures, when the cause of Christ and its tremendous needs have just been permeating the very fibers of her soul?

We have known parents to proudly announce that their children were going to be missionaries someday. But seated at their table, and mingling in the common round of the day, we listened to the casual conversation which set priorities on "things," "standing," "popularity," "what from a worldly standpoint would be considered in vogue," and my husband and I would say to one another, "That child will never go to the mission field." Why? In every conversation the mother and father were imparting their preferences and dropping their hints as to what was acceptable.

A young person was once asked why she had chosen a certain type of hazardous Christian work which was underpaid and for the most part undervalued. "What else could I do," came the response, "when the table conversation was always uplifting those who had undertaken a similar calling?"

The home life of America is being destroyed by divorce; children are being denied the security and feeling of being wanted, having to spend time first with one parent and then the other. The great goal of materialism and high standards is responsible for the motherless homes of America, and the Communists are laughing at our dilemma. They, the Communists, know only too well the powerful influence of a united home upon a generation, and they have long since sworn to destroy that image of such a useful institution. May we be wise before our civilization, like all the ancient ones, goes to ruin having our vitals eaten away by immorality and materialism.

Will you, dear mother, reading this book, deny yourself of some of the ready cash which your work affords you? Will you see further than just today and look ahead to tomorrow with its tragedies when your children will be problems on the State, filling overflowing jails and ruining their constitutions by drug abuse while trying to forget the pangs of a home without a caring parent? Do not bribe them with wonderful gifts at Christmas; it is the day to day little assurances you can give by being in the home, securing that place by prayer and meditation as a shelter from the storms they encounter in the outside world.

A similar survey of Bible knowledge was taken some twenty years ago among students at Westminster College in Pennsylvania, and the results appeared in the *Wesleyan Methodist* magazine. It reiterates the same sad lack of Bible knowledge:

"In an article in *Christianity Today*, written by Joseph M. Hopkins, under the title 'The Fourth R,' is this startling disclosure. Some 357 incoming freshmen were tested on Bible knowledge. A check of six typical questions revealed that:

"256 students could not name the New Testament book which recounts the story of Paul's conversion.

"209 failed to identify correctly the title given the first four New Testament books.

"208 did not know the name of either of Naomi's daughters-in-law.

"173 could not name the first murderer in the Old Testament.

"140 were unable to identify the last book of the Bible.

"129 could not name the author of the largest group of letters in the New Testament.

"Dr. Hopkins, as associate professor at the College, further wrote that 'Of a total of twenty-five questions (most of them elementary), the average number answered correctly was eight! Seventy-five students who had served as Sunday school teachers achieved a median score of eleven.' Most of these students were drawn from upper middle-class Protestant homes. 86 per cent ranked in the upper two-fifths of their high school graduating classes. 60 per cent of these young people were drawn from the sponsoring denominations of the school. 335 of these 357 freshmen identified themselves as communicant members of their respective churches. Most of these students admitted having attended Sunday school from childhood; many reported additional Bible study in vacation church school, released-time classes, summer camps and conferences, as well as personal devotions."

For this child I prayed. . . .

How They Did Pray!

Robert Moffat, the devoted missionary to Africa, knew the value of prayer when he said, "Prayer is the hand that moves the world, but the fingers of that hand are consecrated men and women."

If we were to inquire into the home background of many men and women who were used of God, we would find those consecrated fingers were fathers and mothers bent upon the salvation of their household. We have all heard of the daring adventures of John G. Paton who went to the South Sea Islands, but do we ever think of the prayerful father who impregnated the walls of one small room with his prayers? His son recalls the small Scottish home where those scenes and audible prayers left an indelible impression upon the grown man:

"Our home consisted of a 'but' and a 'ben' and a mid-room, or chamber, called a closet. The one end was my mother's domain, and served all the purposes of dining-room and kitchen and parlor, besides containing two large wooden erections, called by our Scotch peasantry 'box-beds,' not holes in the walls as in cities, but grand, big, airy beds, adorned with many-colored counter panes and hung with natty curtains, showing the skill of the mistress of the house.

"The other end was my father's workshop, filled with five or six stocking frames, whirring with the constant action of five or six pairs of busy hands or feet, and producing right genuine hosiery for the merchants at Hawick and Dumfries. The 'closet' was a very small apartment betwixt the other two, having room in it for a bed, a little table and a chair, with a diminutive window showing diminutive light on the scene. This was the sanctuary of that cottage home. Thither daily and oftentimes a day, generally after each meal, we saw our father retire and shut to the door, and we children got to understand by a sort of spiritual instinct, for the thing was too sacred to talk about, that prayers were being poured out there for us as of old by the High Priest within the veil, within the Most Holy Place.

"We occasionally heard the pathetic echoes of a trembling voice pleading as if for life, and we learned to slip out and in past that door on tiptoe not to disturb the holy colloquy. The outside world might not know, but we knew whence came that happy light as of the newborn smile that always was dawning on my father's face; it was a reflection from the Divine Presence in the consciousness of which he lived. Never in temple or cathedral, on mountain or in glen, can I hope to feel that the Lord God is more near, more visibly walking and talking with men, than under that humble cottage roof of thatch and oaken wattles.

"Though everything else in religion were by some unthinkable catastrophe to be swept out of memory, or blotted from my understanding, my soul would wander back to those early scenes and shut itself up once again in that sanctuary closet, and hearing still the echoes of those cries to God, would hurl back all doubt with the victorious appeal, 'He walked with God, why may not I?' "

Paton's father had been prevented from entering the ministry himself, so he had a strong desire that his own children might fulfill that sacred calling. As Hannah and Elkanah had given up their Samuel to the Lord, so did these descendants of the Covenanters dedicate their children to the service of their beloved Master. The father lived long enough to see his desires fulfilled for three of his sons, John, Walter, and James. They projected their own lives into those of their children, and lived on long after their voice had been silenced in death through the deeds and words of their children who had caught the spirit of their home.

But prayers for one's family outgrow the confines of the home. The father for many years went every night into his little room for intercession, and there, pouring out his heart audibly to God, he knew not that his prayers had been heard by a passerby. John tells the tale: "In long after years the worst woman in the village of Torthorwald, then leading an immoral life but since changed by the grace of God, was known to declare that the only thing that kept her from despair and from the hell of suicide, was when in the dark winter nights she crept close up underneath my father's window, and heard him pleading in family worship that God would convert 'the sinner from the error of wicked ways and polish him as a jewel for the Redeemer's crown.'

" 'I felt,' said she, 'that I was a burden on that good man's heart, and I knew that God would not disappoint him. That thought kept me out of hell and at last led me to the only Saviour.' "

· · · · ·

William Carvosso was from Cornwall, the same southern part of England from which Billy Bray also came. William was converted early in life through Methodist influence, and was tremendously used of God in the salvation of many. But as a father he had influence with his own children. He tells the story: "Returning one night from the quarterly meeting love-feast at Redruth (Cornwall, England), in company with a godly friend, he told me he had the unspeakable happiness the night before to witness the conversion of his young daughter. I informed him I had two children who were getting up to mature age, but I was grieved to say, I had not yet seen any marks of a work of God upon their minds.

"His reply I shall never forget: 'Brother,' says he, 'has not God promised to pour His Spirit upon thy seed and His blessing upon thy offspring?'

"The words went through me in an unaccountable manner; they seemed to take hold of my heart; I felt as if I had not done my duty, and resolved to make a new effort in prayer. I had always prayed for my children; but now I grasped the promise with the hand of faith, and retired daily at special seasons to put the Lord to His Word. I said nothing of what I felt or did, to any-one but the Searcher of hearts, with Whom I wrestled in an agony of prayer.

"About a fortnight after I had been thus engaged with God, being at work in the field, I received a message from my wife, informing me that I was wanted within. When I entered the house, my wife told me, 'Grace is above stairs apparently dis-tressed for something; but nothing can be got from her, but that she must see her father.'

"Judge of my feelings, when I found my daughter weeping penitent at the feet of Jesus. On seeing me she exclaimed, 'O, Father, I am afraid I shall go to hell!' The answer of my full heart was, 'No, glory be to God, I am not afraid of that now.' She said she had felt the load of sin about a fortnight, and that now she longed to find Christ. I pointed her to the true Physi-cian, and she soon found rest through faith in the atoning blood.

"My eldest son had hitherto been utterly careless about the things of God, and associated with youths of a similar disposi-tion of mind; but now he became the subject of a manifest change. He cast off his old companions, and one Sunday after-noon, just before I was going to meet my class, he came to me with a sorrowful mind, and expressed his desire to go with me to the class meeting. He did go and that day cast in his lot with the people of God, and blessed be His holy name, they both continue to this day.

"The work of the Lord prospered more and more in the society. I now began to feel a particular concern for the salvation of my younger son. I laid hold by faith on the same promise which I had before urged, when pleading for my other children, and went to the same place to call upon my God in his behalf.

"One day while I was wrestling with God in mighty prayer for him, these words were applied with power to my mind, 'There shall not a hoof be left behind.' I could pray no more. My prayer was lost in praises, in shouts of joy and 'Glory, glory,

glory! the Lord will save all my family!' While I am writing this, the silent tears flow down from my eyes. His life was quite moral; I could not reprove him for any outward sin. In his leisure hours his delight was in studying different branches of useful knowledge, but this, though good in its place, was not religion. I knew his heart was yet estranged from God.

"After the answer I had in prayer, I waited some time, hoping to see the change effected in him as it was in his sister and brother, but this not taking place according to my expectations, I felt my mind deeply impressed with the duty of embracing the first opportunity of opening my mind to him and talking closely to him about eternal things. I accordingly came to him on one occasion when he was, as usual, engaged with his books. With my heart deeply affected, I asked him if it was not time for him to enter upon a life of religion. I told him with tears that I then felt my body was failing, and that if anything would distress my mind in a dying hour, it would be the thought of closing my eyes in death before I saw him converted to God.

"This effort the Lord was pleased to bless. The truth took hold of his heart. He went with me to the class meeting, and soon obtained the knowledge of salvation by the remission of his sins. This was a matter of great joy and rejoicing to me and my dear wife; we had now the unspeakable happiness of seeing all our dear children converted to God, and traveling in the way to heaven with us."

His children remained true to their Christian profession, the younger one entering upon the ministry and eventually going out as a missionary. It is to him that we are indebted for the biography of his sainted father.

·   ·   ·   ·   ·

I was talking to my twelve-year-old grandson trying to impress upon him that the evil we do not only harms us, but leaves its ugly mark upon our children's children to the third and fourth generation. "But," he said "Grandma, the Bible says that although evil is visited to the third and fourth generation, His mercy is projected to a thousand generations" (Deut. 7:9; Exod. 20:5, 6).

This blessing descending upon our children's children is wonderfully exemplified in the lives of the Talmages. We are all familiar with the sermons of DeWitt Talmage, but how many of us know about the incense of prayer that rose to the Throne of Grace for several generations? Oh, how fraught with lasting blessing are the prayers that rise from caring hearts. The devil certainly has robbed our present generation of that valuable commodity we call "time" that our forebears spent with the Word and in prayer. That little box, the T.V., which the family views by the hour, has filched away the eternal values which held families together in the past. In its place, he has daily conditioned us to present day conditions until we think in terms of worldly enterprise and compromise.

Rev. Dr. Findlay was conducting revival services in the eastern part of the United States in the early part of the nineteenth century. God was working in mighty power, and to these services came a farmer and his wife who lived some ten miles distant. They could only remain for two days, but it was long enough to stir some holy ambitions within them. What could they do for God? They had a family of children—they could start a revival at their farmhouse.

There was a hindrance that evening, as there always seems to be when we determine to win others to Christ. All the children had been invited to a party, and they were excitedly preparing for this grand occasion. Before they left the house, the undaunted mother drew them to her, saying, "Now, you are going to this party. I hope you will have a good time. But remember I am praying for your salvation. I expect to continue in prayer until I hear you come in at the front door."

The mental image of their praying mother haunted the evening at the neighboring party, and there was little enjoyment. The next day as the mother passed through the hallway, she heard Phoebe, her daughter, weeping in her bedroom. She was under deep anxiety of soul. Mother and daughter prayed together until light streamed in like a flood.

But in the meantime, where are the boys? Phoebe knows, for they are in a dreadful state in the barn. The father found David in great agony of mind, and prayed with him until he found peace with God. David Talmage afterwards became the father of Dr. T. DeWitt Talmage, the great orator-preacher. Samuel and Josiah are found, too, and both experience conversion. Samuel later became one of the leading ministers of the South, and became President of Oglethorpe University. And Josiah became a minister of the Gospel.

But David could not keep this wonderful secret to himself. His exuberance knew no bounds, and there was a young woman on a neighboring farm, to whom he must go and pour out his newfound hopes and desires. He ran down the lane where he met Catharine Van Next on the road near her home. As a result of this witness she, too, became a devout Christian.

But a household thus wrought upon could not be kept within doors—soon the whole neighborhood was roused, and at the next Communion service more than two hundred persons joined the church, among them Dr. Talmage's future father and mother. Still the influence does not stop there. David and Catharine were married after a time, and a family of their own gathered about them. Now Catharine remembered how God had answered prayer for her father and mother-in-law, and she determined that her household should witness afresh God's working power. Was not God the same—yesterday—and forever?

So, five mothers gathered in a neighbor's home every Saturday afternoon to pray for the conversion of their children. This holy conspiracy was kept a secret from the family until after her death. But the prayers sincerely offered by those mothers were heard at God's throne, and the children of all those households were converted. Of the eleven children of Catharine's household, her son DeWitt was the last. And he, the only remaining lost sheep, was brought to God through the ministry of a visiting preacher. The family were seated around a glowing fire when the father turned to the minister and asked him to read them a chapter and then pray. The story of the ninety-and-nine and the one lost sheep was read, and then the preacher asked the father if all his children were saved.

"All but DeWitt," the father replied. The minister, gazing into the fire, made graphic the story of the storm, the mountains, the sheep in the fold, the one last lamb, and the shepherd who risked his life to find and bring that one home.

Before the night was out, DeWitt Talmage knew that all the sheep were in the fold, and he the last of the family.

These conversions were not of the "card-signing," "hand-raising," "mental-assent" type, but were born into the kingdom of God with the travail of soul akin to Bible time. Were they short-lived? Let us review several of the family. Phoebe, the sister, became a powerful element for the good of the whole community. In later life, she confused the famous Mr. Talmage more than any other listener, because he said she knew the XYZ of real piety, when he really only knew the ABC's. She died triumphantly after a life of service.

David, DeWitt's father, lived to a good old age, and Divine grace controlled his conversation and actions. He held devotional meetings in his neighborhood, and prayed and sang as enthusiastically to a handful as if he had the thousands listening to him. He visited the sick, buried the dead, and always had a small room for the traveling minister. His biographer says, "For nearly three-quarters of a century he sat in the bower of the promises, plucking the round, ripe clusters of Eshcol. While others bit their tongue for thirst, he stood at the wells of salvation and put his lips to the bucket that came up dripping with the fresh, cool, sparkling waters of eternal life. This joy was not that which breaks in the bursting bubble of the champagne glass, or that which is thrown out with the orange peelings of a midnight bacchanalia, but a lasting joy planted by a Saviour's pardoning grace." All his children but one—a missionary to China—stood at his deathbed watching his triumphant entry into the celestial city.

And what of Catharine, the mother? No divorce played havoc in this Christian home, for God was honored, and fifty-nine years of happiness blessed her union with David. They longed to go together to the celestial city, but Catharine led the way. David wept only once that the family could remember, and that was when he missed "his Catharine."

Ushered into the Kingdom of God through the prayers of his own parents, DeWitt Talmage was impressed enough by the power of prayer to later call together men of God in order to intercede for his own church needs.

"In the winter of 1875, we were worshipping in the Brooklyn Academy of Music in the interregnum of churches. We had the usual great audiences, but I was oppressed beyond measure by the fact that conversions were not more numerous.

"One Tuesday I invited to my house five old, consecrated Christian men—all of them gone now, except Father Pearson, and he, in blindness and old age, is waiting for the Master's call to come up higher. These old men came, not knowing why I had invited them. I took them to the top room of my house. I said to them: 'I have called you here for special prayer. I am in an agony for the great turning to God of the people. We have vast multitudes in attendance, and they are attentive and respectful, but I cannot see that they are saved. Let us kneel down and each one pray, and not leave this room until we are all assured that the blessing will come and has come.' It was a most intense crying unto God. I said, 'Brethren, let this meeting be a secret,' and they said it would be.

"That Tuesday night special service ended. On the following Friday night occurred the usual prayer-meeting. No one knew of what had occurred on Tuesday night, but the meeting was unusually thronged. Men accustomed to pray in public in great composure broke down under emotion. The people were in tears. There were sobs and silences and solemnities of such unusual power that the worshippers looked into each other's faces as much as to say, 'What does all this mean?' And, when the following Sabbath came, although we were in a secular place, over four hundred arose for prayers, and a religious awakening took place that made that winter memorable for time and for eternity. There may be in this building many who were brought to God during that great ingathering, but few of them know that the upper room in my house in Quincy Street, where those five old Christian men poured out their souls before God, was the secret place of thunder."

Background influences count. . . .

How They Prayed in the Family

Women today are vying for equal status with men, and thousands of American women are out working to secure the material advantages which the high standard of living in the West now seems to require. What a price we are paying for such a transfer of women's highest possibilities! A keeper of the home, a guardian of the family, an asset to the church, she has in times past fulfilled a role unparalleled. She has exchanged these for temporal benefits which are fleeting and passing.

Godly women's prayers have supplied the pulpit and the press with some of their finest characters. They have helped the Lord of the harvest to supply missionaries to the countries of the world. They have held up feeble hands of ministering saints. St. Paul realized what an asset Timothy had in both his grandmother and mother. He had already said that for quality he had no man like-minded who would just naturally care for the state of his parishioners. That same unfeigned faith which dwelt first in his grandmother Eunice, was passed on as a heritage to her daughter Lois, and then to the son, Timothy.

The grandfather and maternal grandmother and aunt of Count Zinzendorf had a tremendous influence upon him as a very young child. His grandfather had renounced his estates in Austria and gone into voluntary exile for conscience' sake. Zinzendorf's own father died when he was but six weeks old, and his education was undertaken by his godly grandmother, Baroness Gersdorf, and his aunt. Both of these women were noted for their deep spiritual convictions as well as their learning. Such godly and sacrificial influences had their effect upon the young Count, and at four years of age he dedicated himself to Christ. He, too, renounced his title and estates in young manhood. The world has had to take note of the Moravian settlement on the Count's estate which influenced the world by its daily twenty-four-hour cycle of prayer which resulted in world-wide missionary enterprise.

A poor washerwoman some years ago was compelled by circumstances to take in washings so that the financial needs of the family might be met. As she worked over the tub of hot soapsuds, she would mingle her tears with the lather as she poured out the burden of her heart to God for the salvation of her son. She was not denied, and her boy was born again of the Spirit and became a Sunday school teacher with a concern for his class. One of that class was D. L. Moody, the man who moved multitudes. Edward Kimball, born of prayer, likewise felt a concern for the seventeen-year-old pupil in his class, and pocketing any reluctance he visited the shoe shop where D. L. Moody worked. As a result of this confrontation, Moody that day became a Christian.

How little that humble washerwoman would be praised by an admiring public for her part in Moody's ministry, but the eternal records unerringly will take in all the chains in the link of providence. How interesting it will be to trace the source of all God's working to this mighty weapon of prayer!

Adelia Fiske was a missionary who went out to Persia and worked among the young girls of that nation. She recognized the part her grandmother had played not only in her usefulness, but in that of many of her relatives. She wrote of this grandmother: "Her last days were days of almost continued praying. And the burden of her prayer then was, as it had previously been, that her posterity might be a godly seed even to the last generation." Writing to a cousin, Adelia said: "Have you heard your father tell how she used to pray for her descendants to the end of time?"

Someone took a record of the family and found that in 1857, 300 direct descendants of this godly woman were members of the church. In another letter Miss Fiske said, "I often think I may be receiving blessings in answer to her prayers, for I know she prayed for her children's children for all coming time."

With such a background of prayer, it was little wonder that Adelia Fiske's influence should pervade the students. Their mothers drudged like slaves in the fields all day long and had little time for their homes which were filthy and disordered. The girls indulged in lying and thieving without conscience, and these were to become the mothers of the future. Adelia sacrificed personal liberties and privacy in order to permit the first six students to live in with her.

God did not leave His laborer without His mighty assistance. The Holy Spirit was poured out upon the school, and these girls sought retreats where they could pray into the night hours until salvation purified their lives and outlook. The radius of the influence spread. As many as fifteen women at a time would come to pray into the night hours for the change of heart promised through Calvary. Who but God could induce these darkened souls to desire to pray so earnestly until deliverance from sin came? The prayers of Adelia's ancestors not only prevailed for their families, but for those to whom they would minister.

God made promises to men in the Bible that they would see blessing upon their seed and their seed's seed. Another grandmother up in Canada prayed for all her future posterity that they would fill useful positions in God's great harvest field. She did not live to see her prayers answered, but Africa, India, and the Virgin Islands were ministered to by her grandchildren.

When William Wilberforce was twelve years old, his uncle introduced him to that man of God, John Newton. Unknown to the boy, Mr. Newton felt constantly impressed to bring his name before God in prayer. The results were blessed. An early meeting with God in a personal way, and a consequent growth in grace and in knowledge marked young Wilberforce from that time, although he knew not the secret for fifteen years. John Newton's heart rejoiced when he saw for himself how God answered his prayers.

Wives who know God and pray to Him, have brought abundant blessing to their husbands. One wife prayed for her husband whose business trips took him to far distant countries by plane.

On one trip he was lonely, and an engaging hostess found this rather serious businessman attractive. Using all her arts, she approached him and gave him her phone number in case in his loneliness in a strange city he should desire a woman's company. As he left the plane, she again tried to use her body to attract the business traveler. That night in his hotel room he fought a successful battle with his flesh, and resisted the impulse to phone the attractive air hostess. What had given him the power to resist this strong temptation was the fact that at home, his wife had prayed for him to be kept from all evil when thus alone. Praying women could help avert the tragic separations and divorces which now are so frequent that they are accepted as the normal thing.

In a small village not far from Bedford, England, where Bunyan had been imprisoned, lived a small landholder, Inwood by name, with a family of eight children. Their firstborn was Charles Inwood, who before birth was prayerfully dedicated to the service of the Lord. Surely it was due to the faithful prayers of a godly mother that four out of five sons entered the holy calling of the ministry. Doubtless, there were many days when this busy mother could have complained of boredom as she gave herself to the ever-increasing needs of her growing family. But she had a heritage in her Huguenot ancestry and retained memories of her grandmother, who, though the only educated woman in the village, was singular for her devotion and wonderful prayerfulness.

Charles' memory of his praying mother was expressed in this way: "My mother was distinguished specially by intensity, compassion for all forms of suffering, utter abandonment to the help of all in distress, tremendous will-power, and intense belief in the power of prayer. May her mantle fall on me!"

And we may judge whether or not that mantle enveloped her son throughout his extensive travels, as he preached in many countries of the world and was one of the Keswick speakers at their large camp meetings. In his biography, we read of that prayer habit: "I had a time of wonderful power early in the morning by prayer. . . . It was about four o'clock in the morning and went on till breakfast. So great was the presence of the glory of the Lord that I had to kneel down and with tears of joy adore and glorify God. . . . I mention this because this time of taking hold of God mightily told on my meetings later on. . . . I felt borne along by a mighty current of God and the Holy Ghost.

"I cannot get on with a mere glance at an outline of an address, even where it is an old one. Meditation and prayer with me are a necessity every time I stand up to speak." Cannot you just see the mother's teaching inwrought in the very warp and woof of that man's being? And that mother was projecting herself in her son's public ministry.

If we could interview this saintly mother in the heavenly land, would she regret the days of menial tasks wrought out in obscurity at the wash tub, mending, cooking endless meals, giving hospitality to itinerant ministers? No! Would she not thank God for the times when, tired though she was, she obeyed the impulse to sit down and write a letter to one of her sons assuring him of her prayers? Yes! I am sure she is now partaking in the manifold results of the labors of her children who are so deeply indebted to her for the conversations and prayers which were formative in determining the high principles of godliness which they in turn passed on to a succeeding generation.

James A. Stewart startled a sleeping Europe with the good news of salvation, and saw mighty results. He remembers the time when his mother would steal into their bedroom in the early hours of the morning, and they would hear her pray, "God, save my children." In that great day when reckoning of rewards is made, that mother will share in her son's trophies of grace.

"I cannot tell how much I owe to the solemn words and prayers of my good mother," said Charles Spurgeon. But behind the Training College for young ministerial students, behind the pulpit utterances to huge audiences in the Long Tabernacle, behind the many published books of sermons stands the little figure of a mother who trained her boy in obscurity day in and day out when there were no admiring audiences to applaud her endless task of daily duties.

Right motivation vital for results. . . .

How To Pray for Family Members

William and Catherine Booth had a large family of children, very talented indeed, but all of them engaged in Christian work. Was it a mystery? We quote from one of Catherine Booth's sermons:

"I am afraid a good many professors do not know what the Spirit of intercession means. They do not know anything about the Spirit making intercession for them with groanings that cannot be uttered. When we get more of this Spirit of intercessory prayer in parents, we shall see more spiritual children born. Now, the Holy Spirit says, here we know not what to pray for as we ought, unless the Spirit teaches; hence people are constantly, as James says, asking and not receiving because they ask amiss, 'Ye ask amiss, that ye may consume it upon your lusts'—that means, your earthly desires, affections, purposes, bounded by the horizon of earth.

"I believe in my soul that this is the great reason why thousands of Christians pray and never get answers. They ARE SELFISH IN THEIR PRAYERS; they are earthly; they ask amiss, that they may consume it upon their earthly desires, affections, and propensities. Oh! mothers tell me that they have prayed for their children for years, and not got one of them converted. I say, 'More the pity; more the shame on you.' Why? Because they prayed merely selfish, instinctive prayers, because they were THEIR children, or because they wanted them to be religious, so that they would not go into sin or bring disgrace or misery upon the family, or it would be so nice to have them religious. They don't want them to be righteous over much. They don't want them to be so given up to God as to cut off the vanities and fooleries of this world, and to give themselves up wholly to Christ—that is too much; but just religion enough to make them a comfort to themselves.

"Should you answer such prayers if you were God? Hundreds and thousands of prayers are put up every day that go no deeper and no higher than that, if the motives were analyzed—and God does analyze. He 'searcheth the hearts.' People cannot cheat Him.

"I am afraid many wives pray for their husbands on the same tack. They are not troubled that their husbands are living in disobedience to God, squandering their time, talents, and money, and robbing the kingdom of Christ of what they might be doing for it. The agonizing consideration is, that, if religious, they would spend so much more time at home. They are wasting the money, instead of laying it up for the children. And that, if they were religious, all this would be put right.

"Now, I say, God will never answer that wife's prayer for her husband. You must think of what your husband could be for God—what he could do for God's kingdom—how Jesus Christ has shed His blood for him—how dishonoring a life of sin is to God. You must dwell on this until your heart is ready to break, and you will soon get your husband converted, if you act wisely along with your prayers.

"God will not answer selfish prayers. He hates selfishness—selfishness is the very embodiment of the Devil. You must get out of self; you must look at your child always as God's, as having a precious soul redeemed with the precious blood of Jesus, and having talents and capacities to glorify Him and spread His kingdom. You must ground your prayers on that, and say, 'I would rather lay them in the grave, a thousand times—rather they were poor and despised—than that they should grow up to dishonor Thee.' Then you will get your prayers answered.

"People pray about their businesses. God sees that the way to destroy that man is to let him get on. He does not want to get money in order to roll the old chariot along. God sees that prosperity would eat his soul like a canker, and so He won't let him get on. The Spirit of God never leads the soul to a selfish prayer. No, it leads the soul to weep because men keep not His law, to cry more about His interests than its own. It is willing for its own house to lie desolate, if that will promote the spread of God's kingdom.

"Then comes the last link—faith. Here is another secret. No believer can exercise faith for anything that the Holy Ghost does not lead him up to. You may pray, and pray, but you will never exercise faith until you have the Spirit making intercession in you. There is very little difficulty about believing with people who have taken the three preceding steps. Those who are in fellowship with Jesus, those who are walking in the light, those who have the Holy Ghost as an interceding Spirit—they know what to pray for; they know what the mind of the Spirit is; they know how the Spirit is leading them, and they can march up to the throne and 'ask and receive.'

"They know their request is according to the mind of God, and they can wrestle, if need be, like the Syrophenician woman, if He sees fit to try their faith. He does not always answer at once. He lets them wrestle with groans that cannot be uttered; but they know they will get it, because they know the Spirit is making intercession for them, and they hold on sometime amidst great discouragement and temptation, till the answer comes." —From *Papers on Godliness.*

•   •   •   •   •

From Charles G. Finney we have similar advice:
"Prayer, to be effectual, must be offered from right motives. Prayer should not be selfish, but should be dictated by a supreme regard for the glory of God. A great deal is offered from pure selfishness. Women sometimes pray for their husbands, that they may be converted, because, they say: 'It would be so much more pleasant to have my husband go to church with me,' and all that. And they seem never to lift up their thoughts above self at all. They do not seem to think how their husbands are dishonoring

God by their sins, nor how God would be glorified in their conversion.

"So it is very often with parents. They cannot bear to think that their children should be lost. They pray for them very earnestly indeed. But if you talk with them upon the subject they are very tender about it and tell you how good their children are—how they respect religion, and how they are indeed, 'almost Christians now'; and so they talk as if they were afraid you would hurt their children by simply telling them the truth. They do not think how such amiable and lovely children are dishonoring God by their sins; they are only thinking what a dreadful thing it will be for them to go to hell. Unless their thoughts rise higher than this, their prayers will never prevail with a holy God.

"The temptation to selfish motives is so strong that there is reason to fear a great many parental prayers never rise above the yearnings of parental tenderness. And that is the reason why so many prayers are not answered and why so many praying parents have ungodly children.

"Prayer, to be effectual, must be by the intercession of the Spirit. You never can expect to offer prayer according to the will of God without the Spirit.

"It must be persevering prayer. As a general thing, Christians who have backslidden and lost the spirit of prayer will not get at once into the habit of persevering prayer. Their minds are not in a right state, and they cannot fix their thoughts so as to hold on till the blessing comes. If their minds were in that state in which they would persevere till the answer came, effectual prayer might be offered at once, as well as after praying ever so many times for an object. But they have to pray again and again because their thoughts are so apt to wander away and are so easily diverted from the object.

"Most Christians come up to prevailing prayer by a protracted process. Their minds gradually become filled with anxiety about an object, so that they will even go about their business sighing out their desires to God. Just as the mother whose child is sick goes round her house sighing as if her heart would break. And if she is a praying mother, her sighs are breathed out to God all the day long. If she goes out of the room where her child is, her mind is still on it. If she is asleep, still her thoughts are on it, and she starts in her dreams, thinking that perhaps it may be dying. Her whole mind is absorbed in that sick child. This is the state of mind in which Christians offer prevailing prayer."

•　•　•　•　•

There was another mother living in the South of Ireland whose family of six all labored for God in some capacity. Was it a miracle that this happened? Not only did this unworldly mother pray for her children, but she watched the inroads of the world upon them in their daily life. Many parents wish for their children to be a success in the eyes of the world, and it is little wonder that the children allow the world to dictate their mode of living in later life. Let us look into the conversion of this mother, Harriette Garratt, and the convictions which she adopted in her home. She tells the story herself as related in the biography of her daughter, Helena, by I. R. Govan Stewart.

"It was in the year 1859, the time of the revival in the north of Ireland. I had been very gay—fond of balls, concerts, and all kinds of worldly amusements, not knowing that 'she that liveth in pleasure is dead while she liveth.' However, the time was at hand when the Lord was to step in and begin His work and, 'whatsoever He doeth shall be for ever.'

"My brothers and I happened to go to a Congregational church one morning when the Rev. Denham Smith was preaching. I had not seen the preacher before, but his words struck home to my heart, and for the first time in my life I felt that I had never been born again. It pierced my soul like an arrow, and I could think and talk of nothing else. Then came awful conviction of sin, and I felt myself the most miserable being on the face of the earth; I thought my mind must give way. My friends begged me to go again to amusements, but I *dared* not. I was seeking the Lord, but nowhere could I find Him whom my soul wanted to know and love.

"It was through the verse, 'Trust in the Lord with all thine heart, and lean not to thine own understanding,' that she finally was able to commit herself fully to Christ, and then her joy was as deep as her misery had been, and with wholeheartedness, she left the old way of life for ever. 'Everything must go,' she said—jewelry, ball dresses, everything selfish and extravagant and unlike her Lord. Her joy and happiness were so great that she felt she wanted 'Jesus only'—His smile, His approval, His presence. She spoke to all her friends about Christ, and some of them never forgave her, but she possessed a glorious treasure that she felt she *must* share with others, whether they would hear or whether they would forbear!

"The home at Blackrock, outside of Dublin, was a fine old mansion surrounded by lovely gardens and fields where the herd of Jersey cows grazed that supplied the household with milk, and where Joseph Garratt kept the horses that he loved to drive, like a true Irishman. It was a beautiful home, not only outwardly, but in the harmony of spirit that reigned within. Servants were treated with consideration, but were expected to fill their station—an honorable one—with cheerfulness and faithfulness. The children were devotedly loved and strictly disciplined and commanded to keep 'the way of the Lord.' Visitors were welcomed with Irish hospitality, and one and all were spoken to of the Saviour Who had transformed life for the dear mother—Harriette Garratt. But there was nothing unusual about the home. A ripple of laughter and Irish fun ran through it, and the high-spirited young people found outlet for their energies in tennis, driving, swimming, and music.

"One principle, however, this brave woman insisted on was that of separation from the world—the social order that disdains God. She knew how its fascinating pleasures can deaden spiritual sensitiveness and steal the heart from God, and like Mrs.

William Booth, she covenanted with Him, before they were born, that not one of her children should people hell. Because of the love of hunting and racing in the south of Ireland the boys were not taught riding; nor were they allowed to join a tennis club, though they might bring home as many of their friends as they liked; and the girls were dressed simply in those days of furbelows and frills. She exercised the authority that parents are commanded to exercise over children in their youth, and lived to see every one of them serving God, when they came to years of maturity."

Lonely vigils kept for others. . . .

How Three Women Intercessors Prayed!

While women have not been so much on platforms as their counterparts, still God has often laid the burden upon some obscure woman to intercede for a work that bears the impress of God's anointing. It has often been the partially invalided woman who has been thus set aside to be honored with such a noble calling. When God would use the Faith Mission mightily in the rural districts of Scotland and Ireland, a woman confined to her bed much of the time took seriously the call to join that praying band before His Throne of Grace.

John G. Govan, founder of the Faith Mission, remembers the days of power and prayer: "On looking back, there is one thing that stands out clearly in my mind, and that is the amount of time that we gave to prayer. Prayer became a great joy. We delighted in it. The light of God's countenance and the atmosphere of praise and victory were most refreshing. Whole nights of prayer were then our experience, and many of our Saturday afternoons were given to prayer."

Annie Bowie

Mr. Govan's recollections of his personal acquaintance with one of the Faith Mission's key intercessors, Annie Bowie, were recorded in a 1909 edition of *Bright Words.*

"Twenty-two years ago this month we went for a mission in a little town called Kincardine-on-Forth. A successful series of meetings had just been held at Tillicoultry, in connection with the Y.W.C.A., where we had the hearty help of the late highly-esteemed Mrs. Paton and other earnest Christians. When we announced our intention of attacking Kincardine we were warned that it would be a very hard fight, that there would be little help, etc., etc. But we felt the leading clearly pointed thither. So the writer set forth by the old coach from Alloa, arrived on the Saturday night, and commenced the campaign the next evening.

"The audience that night was considerable, but seemed curious and critical, with not many sympathetic faces. As far as I remember, with the exception of the colporteur, 'no man stood by me' at the start of the work. But before the first week was over there were four conversions, and by the second Sunday two new pilgrims had come to help. What memorable meeting we had that night!

"There was a full hall. Then (as I considered them) immature and inappropriate addresses, followed by about five minutes' appeal for decision for Christ, preceded a glorious after-meeting. Deep conviction and concern seemed to have seized many, and from all over the hall young and old flocked to the penitent form, and with tears of contrition sought the Lord. Thus commenced a glorious revival in Kincardine. The streets were soon resounding with the songs and praises of the young converts, and almost the whole population seemed interested. We were all young and comparatively inexperienced, and to us it was difficult to account for such a manifest work of the Spirit.

"I think it was on the following evening, the Monday, that I received a postcard with the local postmark, which for years I treasured and kept in my Bible. It has disappeared recently, and I do not remember the exact wording. But it was full of praise. 'We have long waited for this' was part of its message, and on different corners were the words, 'Tell it out! Tell it out!' It was quite an inspiration, and we inquired as to who the writer could be. We were directed to a little house in a little square off an obscure street, and there found in bed, in a little room, a suffering saint, one whom we believe to have been one of God's choicest jewels and most faithful servants, Miss Annie Bowie. We found the secret of the blessed work of grace in Kincardine.

"For some time she had known the secret of an overcoming life, the life 'hid with Christ in God.' She had read of it and experienced it, and longed to meet others enjoying the same experience. Some days previously her sister had come into her room, having seen on the streets the Faith Mission bills about a 'free and full salvation,' and announced to her that 'the right people had come to Kincardine at last.' And so we met together in praise, prayer, and fellowship, and a spiritual friendship commenced that has continued throughout these twenty-two years.

"And not only in Kincardine, but in many other places where Faith Mission pilgrims have been enabled to triumph against the forces of darkness, we believe the victory has come largely in answer to prayers that have risen from that bed of weakness.

"During that first five-weeks' mission many blessed hours were spent in that little room in the square, so appropriately named 'Paradise Square,' and distinct spiritual blessing was received by the workers. We never cared to speak much during our visits either then or in succeeding years. There was so much to learn. Miss Bowie had a wonderful knowledge of and a remarkable insight into the Scriptures, and she brought forth many things new and old that have been a help for years, and have been passed on to others with profit. Right through these years she has been deeply interested in and in close touch with the work of the Faith Mission.

"Hers was also very distinctly a life of faith. The household was a delicate one, and, while father and mother were still living, and the former was unable to work, they and the other sister in the house were supported in answer to the prayers and faith of the invalid, and they never lacked. 'He hath dealt bountifully with me' was an expression she often used in her letters. Near the end she told us she 'would rather have a Living Father than a millionaire's bank-book.'

"Praise was very prominent in her spirit and letters. Forty-five years an invalid, the last fifteen of those years never out of her room, poor in this world's goods, weak in her body and often suffering, and yet she was full of thankfulness to her Heavenly

Father for all His goodness to her. Her visitors were greeted with a beautiful smile and words of joy, and her correspondence breathed the spirit of 'In everything give thanks.'

"Though laid aside in weakness, in that little room in an out-of-way town, it could be truly said of her that the world was her parish. She was intelligently interested in and informed of missions and missionaries in many parts of the world. It was customary to find the open Bible lying beside her on the bed along with mission magazines, and motto cards, and around photos of Christian workers, mission maps, etc. Her correspondence used to be large and widespread, and many were the messages of cheer and comfort she sent to busy workers in the great harvest-field. She was able also to give to others out of what was given to her.

"During the last year or two, Miss Bowie got much weaker, and much of her correspondence had to be dropped. In the beginning of February she got much worse, and in the latter part of that month life seemed to be quickly ebbing away. A friend who visited her then wrote that, though 'the struggles for breath were very exhausting and very painful to see, the room was filled with a deep and wonderful peace.' She said the glory to be revealed was as far beyond and above one's thoughts of it as God is above and beyond anyone of us.

"We did not expect to see her again, but she rallied. She asked us if we could call and see her. So it was our privilege once more to meet with her on earth, and have fellowship face to face. Amidst much feebleness, the light and peace and joy of Heaven were realized, and messages were received that will be long treasured. Just a fortnight later, on 19th March, came the telegram, 'Dear Annie face to face with the Master, at rest and satisfied.' Wearying to get home, she yet glorified God in the fires, saying, 'He knows best.' The last sentence she was heard to say, was, 'And then praise Him all the time,' which she repeated twice, and then tried to sing— . . .

'Praise Him, Praise Him, Jesus our blessed Redeemer!'

"And so her lonely life on earth ended in praise. Now she rests from her labors, and her works do follow her."

> Lord, teach us how to pray!
> With prayer to bind the foe,
> With prayer to loosen captive souls
> For whom Thy blood did flow.

> Lord, teach us how to pray!
> With prayer to stand our ground,
> With prayer to weaken Satan's hold
> Where'er his grasp is found.

Ann Cutler

One of William Bramwell's converts, Ann Cutler, was a woman who gave herself to intercession. Abel Stevens in his *History of Methodism* gives us a short history of this remarkable woman. We have noticed in studying biography that when God finds a man given up to His glory alone, He often raises up intercessors for that person. William Bramwell also wrote a short account of Ann Cutler, and we wish we could procure a copy of that book. But may we quote Stevens so that you might share in the higher standards of prayer than are usual in our degenerate day of Christian endeavor.

"Ann Cutler had received the approbation and counsels of Wesley in her public activity among the societies. She was instrumental in the commencement of this great revival, during a visit to Bramwell at Dewsbury. Bramwell, who published an account of her useful life, says: 'She came to see us at Dewsbury where religion had been and was then in a low state. In this circuit numbers had been destroyed through divisions. Ann Cutler joined us in continual prayer to God for a revival of His work. Several, who were the most prejudiced, were suddenly struck, and in agonies groaned for deliverance.

"The work continued almost in every meeting, and sixty persons in and about Dewsbury received sanctification, and walked in that liberty. Our love-feasts began to be crowded, and people from all the neighboring circuits visited us. Great numbers found pardon and some perfect love. The work in a few weeks broke out at Greetland.

"Ann Cutler went over to Birstal, and was there equally blessed in her labors. She went into the Leeds circuit; and, though vital religion had been very low, the Lord made use of her at the beginning of a revival, and the work spread nearly through the circuit. Very often ten, or twenty, or more were saved in one meeting. She and a few more were equally blessed in some parts of the Bradford and Otley circuits. Wherever she went there was an amazing power of God attending her prayers. This was a very great trial to many of us; to see the Lord make use of such simple means, and our usefulness comparatively but small."

Stevens continues his own appraisal of this unusual intercessor: "Ann Cutler seemed not of this world, but rather a pure being descended from Heaven to bless the church in these days of strife. She consecrated herself to a single life, that she might have convenience for public usefulness. 'I am Thine, blessed Jesus,' she wrote in a formal covenant. 'I am wholly Thine! I will have none but Thee. Preserve Thou my soul and body pure in Thy sight. Give me strength to shun every appearance of evil. In my looks keep me pure, in my words pure, a chaste virgin to Christ forever. I promise Thee, upon my bended knee, that if Thou wilt be mine I will be Thine, and cleave to none other in this world. Amen.'

"The sanctity and usefulness of her life would have recommended her, had she been a Papal nun, to the honors of canonization. Her piety rose to a fervid and refined mysticism, but was marred by no serious eccentricity of opinion or conduct. It expressed itself in language remarkable for its transparent and pertinent significance, by diligent but unostentatious religious labors, and a meek and self-possessed demeanor which was characterized by a sort of pensive tenderness and a Divine and tranquil ardor. The example, conversation, and correspondence of Wesley, Perronet, and Fletcher, had raised up a large circle of such consecrated women, and had left with them a fragrant spirit of holiness, which was like ointment poured forth about the altars of Methodism.

"Ann Cutler seldom addressed the people in public: her power was in her prayers, which melted the most hardened assemblies. She was 'instant in prayer.' It was her habit to rise, like the Psalmist, at midnight to call upon God; and the time from her regular morning hour of waking, four o'clock, till five, she spent in 'pleading for herself, the society, the preachers, and the whole church.'

"She died as she had lived. On the morning of her departure she began, before the dawn, to 'ascribe glory to the ever-blessed Trinity,' and continued saying, 'Glory be to the Father, glory be to the Son, and glory be to the Holy Ghost,' for a considerable time. At last looking at her attendants, she exclaimed, 'I am going to die. Glory be to God and the Lamb for ever!' "

To think that the Almighty, perfect in wisdom and holiness, seeks converse with His sinful creatures is beyond our comprehension. But He showed that desire when He told Moses to build Him a sanctuary because He wished to dwell among the people. He never left them—His presence hung over their camp in a cloud by day, and a pillar by night. To partake of such godly wisdom requires time alone when the mind can first be emptied of all, and then can take in from the Ancient of Days, the wisdom by which to work and live.

Today we hurry off from a busy schedule to some weekend seminar on soul-winning, and listen to men who themselves have little time for quiet waiting upon God. It is little wonder that our converts bear our impress rather than that of Him Who is Holy. How it must displease God when He sees the gimmicks, tricks, and attractive displays we employ, hoping thereby to win men to a way of self-denial and cross-bearing. How we need a revival!

Someone once asked Howard Guinness the question, "How long shall I spend in the place of prayer?" He answered, "Time enough to forget time."

> "Faint not, but always pray," the Master said:
>   Not intermittent praying will suffice,
> "Pray, always pray;" then thou shalt have no dread,
>   He never faints who on his God relies.
> Be sure that for thy labors thou shalt reap,
>   If thou faint not, a harvest rich someday:
> And when the Lord rebukes thee, ever keep
>   A steadfast faith: "faint not;" He loves always.
>   —MARGARET T. E. SMITH

Lily Murphy

The periodical, *The Message of Victory*, was going through a very difficult time financially. There had been a period of years in which colporteurs had made a yearly visit upon each subscriber and thus reminded them of the need to renew their subscription. There were therefore thousands of readers on the list who would renew faithfully every year. But now mission policy had changed. No longer could an annual visit be made on everyone, and so, awaiting the usual call, many would ignore the little reminder sent by post. The editor and his wife did not feel they could take them off, and yet, what were they to do? The subscription money was not coming in as it should, and the financial pinch was being felt very keenly. Should they discontinue the magazine?

One morning a letter came in the mail from a Mrs. Murphy of Shotts, Scotland, in which she informed the Harveys that before dawn she was awake and praying that they would be encouraged to keep up the little magazine regardless of pressures otherwise. No one had told this dear soul that the emergency was great as to the future of this bi-monthly magazine. She had been alerted by God to pray for us to continue. A subscriber for some years, she had done all she could to distribute *The Message of Victory* throughout her area. She spoke of her grandchild, who was our youngest distributor, and a picture accompanied the letter. This affirmation of prayer support came again and again, and the many more years which were given to the publishing of *The Message of Victory*, were entirely due to the intercession of this very deep woman of God.

Not only was the publication continued for many years, but God gave wisdom regarding the way in which to print for fewer readers and yet be enabled to meet the large demands of printing costs. A Gospel magazine was incorporated and distributors were raised up, enthusiastic about taking the Gospel into the rural areas, villages, and larger towns and cities of the British Isles. In fact, almost every district was touched with the Gospel over the years because someone had prayed. We owe so very much to our now departed intercessor—Lily Murphy, whose prayers enabled the printed page to go into literally thousands upon thousands of Labor and Conservative clubs, public houses where many congregated at weekends, and homes which were visited in the door-to-door visitation work.

We can say from our hearts with G. Campbell Morgan, that "it seems to us that if the watchers in the heavenly places observe the places of the sons of men amid earth's conflict, those in which they are most interested are the secret places where the saints hold converse with God." That little home in the mining village of Shotts became a shrine to the editor and his wife, for they were blessed by their visits and the times of enriched fellowship with a fellow traveler toward Zion.

"Be all at rest"—for rest is highest service;
    To the still heart God doth His secrets tell:
Thus shalt thou learn to wait and watch and labor,
    Strengthened to bear, since Christ in thee doth dwell.
For what is service but the life of Jesus
    Lived through a vessel of earth's fragile clay;
Loving and giving; poured forth for others;
    "A living sacrifice" from day to day?
                —FREDA HANBURY ALLEN

The prey of the pray-er. . . .

How Praying Women Prevailed!

The following appeared as an article in our periodical, *The Message of Victory,* some years ago and was written by our daughter, Mrs. Trudy Tait.

"For myself," says Daniel Webster, "the greatest argument I know for religion, is an old aunt of mine away up in the New Hampshire hills."

The sentiment has been echoed down the years by many a great and godly man who owed his Christian faith and character to some obscure little woman. Such faithful souls have kept up an incessant barrage of prayer until a wandering prodigal returned to the Father. Nor did they stop there, but kept on praying and witnessing until a life was molded for eternity in the image of the Divine.

In these pages we draw your attention to women such as these, and to the lives they have influenced. This is not merely to sing their praises, but to encourage others who feel their lives are of little count, to pray and keep on praying for a young life whom God has brought under their influence.

Aunt Christina and L. E. Maxwell
(Founder of Prairie Bible College, Canada)

Aunt Christina had begun to pray for Leslie as soon as she knew a child was about to be born into that farm on the golden wheatlands of Kansas. She knew that he would receive no help on his way to Heaven from his parents who lived merely for their money and their grain.

And so this persistent little Scotswoman kept knocking at the door of Heaven on behalf of her rough-and-tumble young nephew whose only companions were uncouth and godless.

When Leslie was a teenager his parents moved into the nearby city where they became the owners of a poolroom. This meant that all his spare time was now spent helping his father in this gambling den. Still Aunt Christina kept her prayers ascending to Heaven, though by this time it must have appeared a human impossibility that Leslie Maxwell would ever become a servant of Jesus Christ.

When, however, Leslie took up full-time employment in the poolroom, his good aunt felt it was time to supplement her prayers by taking positive action. She was determined that the devil should not have it all his own way. And so she persuaded her employers to offer a job to her young nephew, although in reality they had no need of his assistance.

With insufficient money to allow him to live in his former wild manner, Leslie discovered that he could no longer escape the influence of his godly old aunt. Every Sunday he found himself accompanying her to a service. Every week he heard the same plea, "Come to Christ and the church," until these words came to ring in his ears constantly.

For Leslie even to darken a church door was indeed a miracle, for he had grown to utterly abhor the Gospel. What was even still more miraculous was the growing unrest deep within this formerly callous youth. He became utterly convinced that he was heading straight for Hell and on the wrong road entirely.

One night the lad knew he must settle it once and for all. When his roommate was safe asleep the unhappy young man fell on his knees and cried in all sincerity, "O God, forgive my sins." Right there and then Leslie knew that he was indeed forgiven—that he was a new person in Christ Jesus. Aunt Christina's prayers of twenty long years had been answered. Her daily petitions had been heard. Leslie Maxwell was a Christian.

This, however, was only the beginning of the answer. God had a very special future in store for the new convert. He was to become a man of faith and of obedience, and it was to him that God entrusted the founding of the Prairie Bible College of

Canada. This college has been the means of training many young people for a life of full-time service to Christ.

But it all began in the heart of Aunt Christina who, by faith, caught a vision of what her prayers could bring about in a young life.

Miss Barber and Watchman Nee

Miss Barber was having a struggle within herself. God was asking something of her—something that was so costly that she found it difficult to submit. Yet she was desperately afraid to say no. And so she poured it all out to her Heavenly Father. "Lord, I confess I don't like it, but please do not give in to me.—Just wait, Lord, and I will give in to Thee."

A silent witness of this inner conflict was the young Chinese convert, Watchman Nee. He had been invited to join Miss Barber in prayer and, watching her utter honesty and sincerity, he felt convinced that here was a person to whom he could bring his many problems. He knew instinctively that she was someone whom he could safely trust.

And so it happened that, while this faithful and oft-times lonely missionary was not actually instrumental in his conversion, it was from her that Watchman Nee learned many spiritual truths. These he later so ably transmitted by pen and lip to thousands of hungry Christians of both Eastern and Western cultures.

Many were the times, too, when he would pour out his need to this godly soul who always had time to listen to and pray with the many young people who looked to her for spiritual counsel. For example, there was the instance when Watchman Nee felt he just could not continue to work with a Christian brother, two years his senior. To Watchman, an issue was either right or wrong. To his co-worker, his seniority was the judicator in all affairs, and as a result the latter always got his own way.

At last the young man could stand it no longer. He had confided in Miss Barber before concerning this problem, but she had pointed him to the Scripture where the younger was exhorted to obey the elder. But this time he was desperate. He must have a solution. "What annoys me," he protested, "is that that brother has no place for right and wrong." The wise woman of God, looking him straight in the eyes, asked him a point-blank question. "Have you," she asked, "right up to the present moment, never seen what the life of Christ is? Do you not know the meaning of the Cross? These past few months you keep asserting that you do right and your brother is wrong. But do you," she continued, "think it *right* to talk as you have been talking? Do you think it *right* for you to come and report these matters to me? Your judgment of right and wrong may be perfectly sound, but what about your inner senses? Does the life within you not protest against your own resentful behavior?"

Watchman Nee was astounded by such a reply, but the Holy Spirit within witnessed that while his logic may have been perfectly sound, his own spirit had not been a right one.

This was only one of the many lessons learned from this dear saint who so lived in solitude with her God that she knew His mind and His will, and could thus wisely instruct others. There were times, however, when even her young friend could scarcely understand her seeming lack of activity. With the impatience of youth he would urge her to go out into the world with her teaching and experience. It was such a pity, he would tell her, that she should remain so secluded. Why didn't she go out and *do* something?

But Miss Barber knew better. Doubtless, through the eye of faith, she caught a vision of the potential of the young folks who so often sought her out. She had discovered the secret learned by other saints, that prayer is the work, and for ten long years had interceded for young Chinese men. She realized the privilege of being an instrument through which the Holy Spirit could forge a life for eternity, laying a foundation of truth, and being instant in prayer. More would thus be accomplished for eternity than hundreds of sermons and multiplied activity performed without the backing of the Divine.

And so it was not surprising that Watchman Nee described her thus: "I always thought of her as a 'lighted Christian.' If I did but walk into her room, I was brought immediately to a sense of God." He adds a further insight into her character: "I was very young and had lots of plans, lots of schemes for the Lord to sanction. . . . With all these I came to her to try and persuade her. . . . But before I could open my mouth she would say a few quite ordinary things . . . and light dawned. It simply put me to shame. My scheming was all so natural, so full of man, whereas here was one who lived for God alone. I had to cry to Him, 'Lord, teach me to walk that way.' "

As those who have read his books will realize, God indeed did teach Watchman Nee to "walk that way." And it was the example and prayer of this one devoted missionary that did so much to reveal to this young man what the crucified life really meant. It was also from her ample bookshelves that Watchman found great help. Thus, through the writings of godly men, truths were planted within him which he, in turn, has so wonderfully and scripturally portrayed in books such as *The Normal Christian Life,* and many others.

And thus it is to Miss Barber that we, who so love his books, owe so very much. May her influence which lives on down the passing years, inspire many a faithful missionary, called to a similar life of prayer and intercession. God needs them, young converts depend upon them, and a world will bear the effect of their God-given, Spirit-filled lives.

Betty Lee, the Landlady, and her Lodger, Charles Champness

I am quite certain that not many will have ever heard or known of Betty Lee. She, however, was the landlady who one day asked her young lodger, Charles Champness, to go and hear George Osborn preach. Later one of the lodger's sons, Thomas, became the founder of Cliff College and was the first editor of the paper entitled *Joyful News.* Josiah Mee, the biographer of Thomas Champness, tells how far-reaching was this single act of an obscure landlady:

"Always remembering that his father was led to the house of God by the kind efforts of an old lady with whom he lodged during his early weeks in Lancashire, Mr. Champness was fond of showing how much might follow some such effort to induce men to go and hear the preaching of the Gospel. 'Betty Lee,' he used to say, 'has fairly earned the right to a place in the chronicles of God's church. She little thought that her lodger would have three sons who would be preachers of the Gospel, and that among their converts would be ministers and evangelists in this and other lands, whose spiritual children would be numbered by thousands.' We may well believe that, having now met her in the paradise of God, he has saluted the old saint who began all this work by just asking her new lodger to go and hear young George Osborn preach."

Three Women and Brownlow North—the Scottish Evangelist

Although Brownlow North was such a notorious playboy, he was fortunate to have the acquaintance of three godly women. These three prayed long years that he might be brought out of his wild and wicked life into the purity and holiness of true Christianity.

The first to have influenced Mr. North was his mother, who was a devoted follower of Christ. She it was who doubtless prayed the longest for him and, loving him the most, wept most over his neglect of God. She it was, too, who, when he finally came under a deep sense of sin and even despaired of ever being changed, said to him with conviction, "Brownlow, God is not only able to save you, but to make you more conspicuous for good than ever you were for evil!"

Then there was the godly Duchess of Gordon, who had been asked by some of Mr. North's friends to try to get him away from his evil companions. Once, therefore, when he was in the area, she invited him to dinner. During the meal, her guest turned suddenly and asked her gravely, "Duchess, what should a man do who has often prayed to God and never been answered?"

With a silent prayer for help, the hostess, looking him in the eye, answered, "Ye ask, and receive not, because ye ask amiss, that ye might consume it on your own lusts" (James 4:3). Brownlow North's face changed color, and not another word did he say until he was leaving, when he thanked the Duchess and seemed greatly touched.

In fact, it was this incident, together with the severe illness of his son, that so softened this godless man's heart that he entered Oxford, took a degree, and was about to enter the ministry. Then it was that news of his previous escapades reached the ears of the Bishop who was about to ordain him.

"Mr. North," the Bishop addressed him, "if I were in your position and you in mine, would you ordain me?"

"My Lord, I would not," was the candid reply.

And so Brownlow North never did become a clergyman. Instead he plunged once more into his old dissolute life and became even wilder and more licentious than before.

Meanwhile yet another godly lady was remembering this seemingly hopeless case before her Heavenly Father. She it was to whom his wife turned for help when one evening, while playing cards as usual, her husband was suddenly struck with a terrible illness. This Miss Gordon, having been summoned so suddenly, came post haste to Brownlow's home. She was met by the sick man who greeted her with the words, "I am, dear auntie, I trust, by the grace of God, a changed man, and I have been writing to some of my former companions to tell them of the change."

Then she discovered that one evening while playing cards he had been struck very ill—so ill that he was sure he was going to die. He became seized with a conviction that he was not ready for the future, and that if he did not pray then he would never have another chance to do so. Sick as he was, however, his pride kept him back for a long time. How could he kneel down and pray to God in front of the servant girl who was lighting the fire? But at last, in utter desperation, and feeling certain he would die very soon, he threw himself on his knees and cried for mercy.

It was after this that there was a distinct change in him. He did not die, though for weeks he lived in torment, battling with Satan who tried to fill him with doubts—doubts that God existed—fears that he was at any rate too wicked to ever be saved.

It was only the prayers of his dear mother and Miss Gordon and others that helped him through this terrible conflict of soul. At one period he would walk up and down the garden like one demented, reiterating the words, "God is. There is a God," in reply to the continuous whispering of his former master, the devil.

At length, however, this much prayed-for man was completely delivered from all doubts, fears, habits, and all his former vices. He was utterly and wholly transformed.

He eventually traveled up and down Scotland telling of what the living Christ had done for him, and making clear the Gospel to hundreds.

He always marveled that God should have bothered to save and to use someone with such a record as he. There he was, a man in his forties, with plenty of money and friends and with no thought of God or Heaven—suddenly struck ill—an illness that could not be treated medically—and then receiving a revelation of his sin, and finally wonderfully delivered, and then called to be His servant! What explanation can be given? God's love—yes; and the faithful, incessant prayers of three women. That was the secret!

Cousin Polly and Paget Wilkes
(Co-founder of the Japan Evangelistic Band)

Cousin Polly, a frail little lady from South Africa, spent hours together in prayer. She had a very special burden for the careless, light-hearted teenager, Paget Wilkes.

It was not, however, until four years later that this same young man, now twenty-one years of age, became a real out-and-out Christian. This occurred just before he entered Oxford University.

Perhaps Cousin Polly had been given a special insight from God into what this man would someday become. For Paget

Wilkes was called to be a missionary in Japan under Barclay Buxton, and was greatly instrumental in founding the Japan Evangelistic Band.

His writings and poems have been especially helpful to many. It all began, however, with the frail little lady who interceded until an answer came.

Aunt Sarah and Colonel Ingersoll

We conclude with an excerpt from the life of the famous infidel, Colonel Ingersoll, trusting and praying that it will make our readers realize that the crying need of our world today is a praying, loving, interceding, Christian womanhood.

"Colonel Ingersoll was notorious as an infidel. His attacks on the Bible were severe, but not serious, because the old Book stands. He had a godly aunt, of whom he was very fond. She was 'a living epistle.' The colonel wrote a book antagonistic to the Christian faith. He forwarded a copy to his aunt, and on the fly-leaf he wrote these words: 'If all Christians had lived like Aunt Sarah, perhaps this book would never have been written.' There would be fewer infidels if there were more true Christians living Christlike lives."

There is a place where thou canst touch the eyes
Of blinded men, to instant, perfect sight;
There is a place where thou canst say "Arise!"
To dying captives, bound in chains of night.
There is a place where thou canst reach the store
Of hoarded gold, and free it for the Lord;
Where thou canst send the worker or the Word;
There is a place where Heaven's restless power
Responsive moves to thine insistent plea;
There is a place—a silent, trusting hour—
When God Himself descends and fights for thee;
Where is that blessed place, dost thou ask "Where?"
O soul, it is the secret place of prayer.

—ADELAIDE PROCTOR

Three wives receive an answer. . . .

How They Prayed for Their Husbands!

S. D. Gordon, the prolific writer of books, has recorded a striking incident of a wife who prayed for her skeptic husband and was heard.

"Out in one of the trans-Mississippi States I ran across an illustration of prayer in real life that caught me at once, and has greatly helped me in understanding prayer. If one could know all that is going on around him, how surprised and startled he would be. If we could get *all* the facts in any one incident, and get them colorlessly, and have the judgment to sift and analyze accurately, what fascinating instances of the power of prayer would be disclosed.

"There is a double side to this story. The side of the man who was changed and the side of the woman who prayed. He is a New Englander, by birth and breeding, now living in this Western State: almost a giant physically, keen mentally, a lawyer, and a natural leader. He had the conviction as a boy that if he became a Christian he was to preach. But he grew up a skeptic, read up and lectured on skeptical subjects. He was the Representative of a district of his Western home State, in Congress; in his fourth term or so I think at this time.

"The experience I am telling came during that Congress when the Hayes-Tilden controversy was up, the intensest Congress Washington had known since the Civil War. It was not a time specially suited to meditation about God in the halls of Congress. And further, he said to me that somehow he knew all the other skeptics who were in the Lower House, and they drifted together a good bit and strengthened each other by their talk.

"One day as he was in his seat in the Lower House, in the midst of the business of the hour, there came to him a conviction that God—the God in Whom he did not believe, Whose existence he could keenly disprove—God was right there above his head thinking about him, and displeased at the way he was behaving towards Him. And he said to himself: 'This is ridiculous, absurd. I've been working too hard; confined too closely; my mind is getting morbid. I'll go out, and get some fresh air, and shake myself.' And so he did. But the conviction only deepened and intensified. Day by day it grew. And that went on for weeks, into the fourth month as I recall his words. Then he planned to return home to attend to some business matters, and to attend to some preliminaries for securing the nomination for the Governorship of his State. He was in a fair way to securing the nomination.

"He hardly reached his home before he found that his wife and two others had entered into a holy compact of prayer for his conversion, and had been so praying for some months. Instantly he thought of his peculiar, unwelcome Washington experience, and became intensely interested. But not wishing them to know of his interest, he asked carelessly when 'this thing began.' His wife told him the day. He did some quick mental figuring, and he said to me, 'I knew almost instantly that the day she named fitted into the calendar with the coming of that conviction or impression about God's presence.'

"He was greatly startled. He wanted to be thoroughly honest in all his thinking. And he said he knew that if a single fact of that sort could be established, of prayer producing such results, it carried the whole Christian scheme of belief with it. And he did some stiff fighting within. Had he been wrong all those years? He sifted the matter back and forth as a lawyer would the evidence in any case. And he said to me, 'As an honest man I was compelled to admit the facts, and I believe I might have been led to Christ that very night.'

"A few nights later he knelt at the altar in the Methodist meeting-house in his home town, and surrendered his strong will to God. Then the early conviction of his boyhood came back. He was to preach the Gospel. He utterly changed his life, and has been preaching the Gospel with power ever since.

"Then I was intensely fascinated in getting the other side, the praying-side of the story. His wife had been a Christian for years, since before their marriage. But at some meetings in the home church she was led into a new, a full surrender to Jesus Christ as Master, and had experienced a new consciousness of the Holy Spirit's presence and power. Almost at once came a new intense desire for her husband's conversion.

"As she prayed that night after retiring to her sleeping apartment, she was in great distress of mind in thinking and praying for him. She could get no rest from the intense distress. At length she rose and knelt by the bedside to pray. As she was praying and distressed, a voice, an exquisitely quiet inner voice, said, 'Will you abide the consequences?' She was startled. Such a thing was wholly new to her. She did not know what it meant, and without paying any attention to it, went on praying. Again came the same quietly spoken words to her ear, 'Will you abide the consequences?' And again the half-frightened feeling. She slipped back to bed to sleep. But sleep did not come. And back again to her knees, and again the patient, quiet voice.

"This time with an earnestness bearing the impress of her agony, she said, 'Lord, I will abide any consequence that may come if only my husband may be brought to Thee.' And at once the distress slipped away, and a new sweet peace filled her being, and sleep quickly came. And while she prayed on for weeks and months patiently, persistently, day by day the distress was gone, the sweet peace remained in the assurance that the result was coming.

"What was the consequence to her? She was a Congressman's wife. She would likely have been, so far as such matters may be judged, the wife of the Governor of her State, the first lady socially of the State. She is a Methodist minister's wife, changing her home every few years. No woman will be indifferent to the social difference involved. Yet rarely have I met a woman with more of that fine beauty which the peace of God brings, in her glad face, and in her winsome smile.

"Do you see the simple philosophy of that experience? Her surrender gave God a clear channel into that man's will. When the roadway was cleared, her prayer was a spirit-force traversing the hundreds of intervening miles, and affecting the spirit-filled atmosphere of His presence."

The biographer of Mrs. Catherine Booth, F. Booth-Tucker, records how Catherine's mother, Mrs. Mumford, prayed long and fervently for her husband. "Long into the nights she would pray for him, and indeed made it the goal of her existence to win him back to the blessed experiences of the past. At length, after a season of sorrow which left its life-mark upon her, prayer was answered, and Mr. Mumford returned from the pursuits and pleasures of the world to find his satisfaction in higher things. True, he was not what he had been when Sarah Milward first met him—the fiery, enthusiastic preacher of salvation with whom she had fallen so spontaneously in love. Nevertheless, the change was great and was hailed with joy."

• • • • •

An article written anonymously but from a well-known pen came to our attention some years ago. For many years this husband and father had been prayed for, but there was no response. Finally, the mother asked her children to meet with her at the Mercy Seat at a certain hour daily. Then it seemed the Holy Spirit inspired a prayer in the mother's heart, and something happened after forty years. The following was written by one of the children whose name was withheld.

"Whatever may have been the mental state of him who was the object of our concern, there was a growing feeling of intensity in our mother. Her spirit had no rest.

"After they had retired one night, she said a few words expressive of her concern for him. He gave her an indifferent answer and fell asleep.

"She arose, in the fullness of an anxious heart, returned to the sitting room, raked open a bed of coals, and spent the night in prayer. It was cold, being the latter part of February. Behold the difference between the believer and the unbeliever. The one sleeps over his own impending ruin; the other wakes and wrestles for him in agonizing prayer.

"As the day dawned, she fell into a train of reflections like the following:

" 'I have borne this burden forty years. I can carry it no farther; it is too heavy for me; I must roll it off on God. I feel that I have done. I cannot convert his heart, however much I distress myself. Perhaps I have sinned in distressing myself as I have been doing.

" 'God may have seen in me the want of a simple reliance upon Him or of true and absolute submission to His will. He may have seen me unwilling or afraid to commit the matter of my husband's salvation *entirely* to Him. But I feel that I *must* and *do* thus commit it to Him now. I will afflict myself no more. I shall still pray for him and use such means as may seem advisable, but—saved or lost—I leave the result with God.'

"She was conscious of a simplicity of trust now, and of a relief of mind such as, on that subject, she never had felt before. So she prayed and found relief like the wife of Elkanah. In the morning after breakfast, finding him alone, she said a few words to him to this effect. She remarked that they had lived together above forty years; that their union had been an affectionate and happy one, and that it was painful to think they soon were to be separated without any prospect of ever being reunited.

" 'And now I have this one request to make: Devote this day to the concerns of your soul; devote it to reflection and to prayer. If you cannot do it for your own sake, do it to oblige me.'

"Struck with her earnest manner, he said decisively, 'I will.' He was 'not able to resist the wisdom and the spirit' with which she spoke.

"She saw no more of him until night, when he came in and sat down, sad and thoughtful, by the fire. No allusion was made to the interview of the morning. It was evident that he was not happy. He had an eye more expressive of sorrow than any eye I ever saw. It glistened but did not flow with tears, and its color seemed to deepen. Sorrow was in him a sealed fountain; it found no vent in words. The next day he again disappeared and was gone till evening. His countenance and manner when he returned were still thoughtful, but there was a serenity in his look which was not there before.

" 'I do not know,' said he to my mother, 'what has ailed me today. My feelings have been unusual and, indeed, very strange.'

" 'Why, how have you felt?' she asked.

" 'I can hardly tell you,' he replied. 'I have no reason to think myself a Christian—or, perhaps, that I ever shall be. But it has seemed to me this afternoon as if everything was changed. All nature appeared to speak of God. The trees, the hills, the skies—everything seemed to praise Him. And I felt that I loved everybody. If there is anyone that I have hated, it is Mr. G____ (a certain revivalist, the particular type of whose zeal or tactics had disgusted him); but I have felt today that I loved him like a brother.'

"It was afterward known that he spent the first of those two days in a retired valley on his farm and the other in a wood. He had engaged to spend one day in retirement. It might have appeared that he did that merely to fulfill a promise. The second day was eminently probationary and eminently critical.

"On the following morning the minister, knowing nothing of my father's state of mind, happened to call. They had a long conversation together. On leaving the house, the minister said to the first Christian he met, 'I have great news to tell you; Mr. ____ has become a new man. I have just come from conversing with him, and I have no doubt of the reality of his conversion to Christ.' After suitable delay and self-examination, my father made a public profession of his faith, receiving baptism in connection with that act. He lived ten years to prove the genuineness of his faith, and died at the age of seventy-five."

Two husbands remained unmoved. . . .

How Marriage Partners Prayed!

In the previous chapter we have related instances of where the prayers of wives prevailed for their husbands, but there is the great unanswered "why?" for those who have prayed and been most used of God, and still their partners remained obdurate for many years, even dying in an unrepentant state. It may be that those wives did not feel that the Holy Spirit inspired such a prayer in their hearts, for the Scripture says that we know not how to pray as we ought. The Spirit, knowing the mind of God, groans within the suppliant, making that kind of prayer possible. Perhaps those wives saw that it was their particular cross, and that incompatibility in marriage was the shaping instrument in the hands of their loving God to refine, purify, and mold them into Christ-likeness.

There were several outstanding women in the early days of Methodism in the United States—Mother Cobb, and Aunty Coon. Each had unbelieving husbands who, as far as we can recall, never attained to grace so that unity of purpose was achieved.

•   •   •   •   •

Mother Cobb's husband had once been somewhat active in the church, but he had grown cold and drifted away. He did not understand the fervor and zeal with which his wife served the Lord, and thought perhaps if he could separate her from her circle of believing friends in New York he would thus quench her enthusiasm for God. So they moved west and settled in a sparsely populated area in Illinois. Little did the husband realize that the flame burned within her own heart, and was not dependent upon her like-minded friends, but even blazed forth the brighter because of the coldness round her.

This saintly woman, whose labors were so greatly owned of God in revival, never allowed her husband's indifference to cause her to be remiss in untiring efforts in personal visitation and prayer with the sick. For thirty years she tramped the roads and lanes of both town and country, visiting the afflicted and interceding at the Throne of Grace for special series of meetings held in the surrounding area.

So intimate was her relationship with her heavenly Father that He revealed to her some of His secrets. "Shall I hide from Abraham that thing which I do?" said the Lord about His loved servant Abraham. Mother Cobb was given an intimation regarding a coming revival in her area. After the revival she said to some of her friends: "My dear sisters, the Lord showed me that we must go to the red school house and begin meetings. I saw them flocking there from the east and from the west, and the north and the south." And so it had been.

Again she wrote: "Perhaps we do not think enough of prayer—intercessory prayer, direct appeals by names for others, laying their needs—all we desire for them, out before God. We do not believe as we should. Now it would help those we serve, penetrating the heart we cannot open, shielding those we cannot speak to, comforting where our words have not power to soothe, following the steps of our beloved through the toils and perplexities of the day, lifting off their burdens with an unseen hand. At night no ministry is so like an angel's as this—silent, invisible, known but to God. Through us descends the blessing, and in Him alone ascends the thanksgiving. Surely not any employment brings us so near to God as earnest, sincere prayer. There is a depth of wisdom in the words: 'If only we spoke more to God for men, than even to man for God.' Lord, teach us to pray!"

In the above we see that this dear woman intercessor grasped the ministry of prayer as God designed it should be. Isaiah portrays the kind of prayer and fasting which is pleasing to God. Not for pleasure, must we intercede; not to smite with the fist of wickedness; not to make our voice to be heard on high; not to pray so that we appear before others more holy than we really are. But "is not this the fast that I have chosen? to loose the bands of wickedness, to undo the heavy burdens, and to let the oppressed go free, and that ye break every yoke? Is it not to deal thy bread to the hungry, and that thou bring the poor that are cast out to thy house? when thou seest the naked, that thou cover him; and that thou hide not thyself from thine own flesh?" (Isa. 58:6, 7).

There seemed to be times when God humored this dear saint. Her home was at one time invaded by mice, but nothing seemed too small or insignificant to take to the Lord Who knows the sparrow's fall and also knows the number of the hairs of our head. "I came home," she notes, "and found the mice had gotten into the house. They were in the pantry and in the clothes, and all over the house. They did distress me so that I went to my knees and asked Jesus to send them away, and every one of them left."

Doubtless God would not have thus answered had this servant of His not been so constantly away from home on rounds of calling on the sick and afflicted. He would have expected her to use the means at hand to rid her home of these rodents.

Thirty years of faithful effort had this diligent soul-winner and intercessor spent sowing throughout the district so that when the evangelist, Mr. Redfield, came to their area, he found a harvest ready for reaping, But Mr. Redfield, though used very extensively by God throughout the United States, and with no uncertain call to his work, was given a thorn in the flesh in his married life. "E'en though it be a cross that raiseth me," he could well say, for he had little conjugal happiness.

•　•　•　•　•

Aunty Coon, a Free Methodist, at an early age was strongly influenced by her parents to marry a judge older than herself. The man's persistency in desiring marriage finally decided the course for the not-too-willing daughter. She was tied to a man who, though he seemed in a way to love her, lived a dissolute life and almost broke her heart.

This unfortunate wife was later greatly helped by Mother Cobb, and God took hold of her life in a mighty way, using her gifts of discernment to help the ministers whom she assisted. Mother Cobb had approached Aunty Coon and challenged her with the following words: "God makes me feel that you must be a soul-winner, and He will take away entirely the fear of man from you. We are waiting for you. There are many standing back of you, and unless you yield they will be lost."

Aunty Coon felt that perhaps Mother Cobb did not understand her home situation with an unbelieving husband. "As I told her with tears," said Aunty Coon, "of the opposition I must meet at home, that probably would continue all my life-time, she would say, 'I know about such a life. God, Who has called you, will help you; there is a way through, my dear.'"

Aunty Coon never looked back, and great was the support she rendered by her presence in many a series of services held throughout the country. Here she was specially used in the work of dealing with seekers. Her discernment seemed to penetrate right down to the need which others knew nothing about. So God often remunerates the wives who meet with constant coldness in their home life. Through this dear woman's influence, Vivian A. Dake was led into a deeper experience and consecration to the work of God, and went through the land as a blazing meteor for a number of years, turning many to righteousness, and marshalling a Spirit-baptized army to fight manfully the battles of the Lord. He died at a comparatively early age after being much used of God in this way.

"The king's heart is in the hand of the Lord, as the rivers of water: he turneth it whithersoever he will" (Prov. 21:1).

How the Veiled Empress Prayed!

There have been times when the destiny of nations has depended upon some obscure woman entrusted with the exalted task of rearing a son who would one day rule an empire, wisely making decisions which would make an impact upon the world.

The Bible records several instances where, long before the need arose, God had in His foresight prepared a future statesman or prophet to meet the exigency of the hour. Take for example Samson, a mighty warrior and judge in the Bible. God made His will known to the parents and gave them directives as to his training.

Hannah was allowed to endure the reproaches of her rival, Peninnah, stinging her into a state of prayer which amounted to soul travail. When, in answer to her agonizing prayer, a son was given, he was dedicated to God and trained in the temple at a very young age. Her son was the last of the long line of judges whom God had chosen to rule Israel. He tided the nation over a most difficult period of transition when the judges, chosen by God, were rejected, and a king was desired in order that they might imitate the heathen nations round about. Samuel warned the people in God's name of the dire consequences of rejecting the invisible Leader, Who had guided them successfully through the conquest of Canaan, in order to choose a king who would go before their armies with chariots of iron and strength of armed men.

A harem is not exactly the most propitious place in which to be a witness for God. But Queen Esther's story in Scripture is an amazing episode of how an orphan girl was chosen to be one of the many wives of an oriental ruler, and served God so effectually in her position that she was the means of saving the lives of many of her Jewish people.

The following story is just as amazing a providence, in which it would seem that God used two orphan girls from Martinique, brought up as Christians, to influence foreign courts and help to decide the destiny of nations.

"My name is Marie Marthe Aimee Dubuc de Rivery, and I was born in 1765 on a sugar plantation, La Pointe Royale, in Martinique. This belongs to the beautiful group comprising the West Indies. It is under French rule, and my parents were both French.

"I lost my father when I was a tiny baby, and my mother followed him in death before I was six years of age. The gentleman who became my guardian was very kind and gave me the best of care. My nurse was a devoted colored woman whom I called Da.

"My cousin Josephine was my best friend. I loved her dearly. Although so closely related, we contrasted one another sharply in appearance. Her hair and eyes were dark, while I had golden hair and blue eyes. As Josephine and I talked and laughed and played together, life seemed very bright. Every need that we had was supplied. Our island home was indeed a beautiful spot, with its bright-hued vegetation.

"In 1776 I was sent to France to finish my education. My teachers praised my ability as a student.

"When I was twenty-one I set out for my homeland. After a few days of sailing, our vessel was attacked by Algerian corsairs. They won in the fight that ensued, and we passengers of the ship were made prisoners. The old pirate chieftain was attracted by my blue eyes and golden hair and decided to send me as a gift to his master, the bey of Algiers. My personal feelings were not considered; I was simply a woman and a slave.

"When I stood before the bey of Algiers he, in turn, thought it would be a good idea to send me as sort of an appeasement gift to the Sultan of Turkey. Accordingly, I was fitted out with a wardrobe such as would be appropriate to the ruler of the Ottoman Empire. Then I set sail. During this long voyage every comfort was allowed me. Sometimes I almost prayed for death; again, a determination would sweep over me to show the infidel Turks what a woman was like who had been brought up under the benefits of Christian civilization. At least, I told myself, I never would renounce my religion. There was no one with whom I could talk things over, for the others on board did not know my language, nor did I know theirs. So I suffered in silence.

"Then, one day, a vision of golden towers and mosques appeared before my startled eyes. My voyage was over, and I stood on the brink of a new life. Everything seemed most unreal to me as I stepped on shore. Proceeding toward the High Gate, I was so shocked at the sight which confronted me that I almost fell over in a faint. Men's heads were impaled on the gate; they had been severed so recently that blood still was dripping from them.

"The Sultan accepted me as a gift from the bey, and the friendship between the two was renewed and cemented thereby. I was given quarters in the Seraglio, the palace of the Sultan; this was to be my future home. The Seraglio was a city in itself. It was capacious enough to house twenty thousand persons.

"The ruler of Turkey, I knew, held complete sway over his subjects—body and soul. Nevertheless, I made up my mind that I would die rather than lose my faith in God and be plunged into spiritual darkness.

"My son was born July 20, 1785. I named him Mahmud. His hair and eyes were dark like his father's. How carefully I guarded my little one! As soon as he was old enough to under-stand, I began to pour into his ears the truths which I had believed all my life.

"My mind, on account of the Western teachings and ideals with which I had been inculcated, was clear in its grasp of the intrigues of the palace. I found it a veritable political battle-ground. There were persons, I learned, who stood between my son and the throne.

"Once a month I held audience for the women of the court. On such occasions, however, I always sat behind a lattice. Because I was such a contrast in complexion to those about me, I did not wish to be seen more than was necessary. The greatest difference of all, of course, lay in our religion. I began to love these women and to feel a concern for the people of Turkey in general. I determined that should my son ascend the throne and my life be spared, I would help them all I could.

"My guardian finally learned of my whereabouts, and we were able to carry on a correspondence. He told me that my cousin Josephine had married Napoleon Bonaparte and had become the Empress of France.

"On July 28, 1808, my son Mahmud became the ruler of Turkey. The influences which I had thrown around him from his childhood had by this time become a part of his very being. I knew he would not be a despotic ruler as his predecessors had been.

"As I thought of Josephine in her high station, and of myself in my unbelievable role, a wave of homesickness for our island home swept over me. But I quickly dismissed it, confident it was none other than Providence that had placed each of us in her allotted sphere. Josephine and I exchanged letters, as our comradeship could be renewed only in this way. Napoleon wrote to Mahmud, desiring his friendship and military aid. Would Mahmud lend him troops for the proposed campaign into Russia?

"My son came to me in my garden; he desired advice at this crucial time. We earnestly discussed the matter, walking to and fro along the narrow paths. Napoleon little guessed that the answers to his letters were dictated by a woman. Of course, they bore my son's signature, but the thoughts expressed were mine. I can truly say that, in the advice I gave, I had the interest of France at heart.

"Word reached me that Napoleon had divorced Josephine, who had so tenderly loved and so faithfully aided him in the hard days before his success. I knew that such action was not right; all my religious teachings of the past rose up in rebellion against it. Mahmud and I again walked in the garden the evening after I had received the sad message, and I confided it to him. He said little, but I know he felt that anything which hurt his mother so was wrong and hence not to be passed over lightly. When Mahmud left me and returned to his room, another communication from Napoleon lay on his table. He read it with a frown. Already he had made a promise, but our talk in the garden now stood between him and its fulfillment.

"'Napoleon has been untrue to my mother's ideals,' he thought. 'How can I trust him? If I enter into an alliance with him, what may he not do to me?'

"And so the promise never was kept; Mahmud did not send troops to aid Napoleon in his Russian campaign. History records the dreadful failure of that campaign. The crestfallen French soldiers, caught in the deadly grip of a Russian winter, struggled back toward home as best they could. Thousands of them froze to death. Perhaps, if I had more fully understood the situation, I might have tried to persuade my son to keep his word on this occasion; for to me a promise is a sacred thing. But it is useless to ponder over that now.

"I saw many badly needed reforms accomplished in Turkey through my son. The secret of my influence over him was the more easily kept because theoretically, the mother of a sultan is of no consequence whatever. Indeed, she is considered a slave.

"Someone, however, who evidently understood the true state of affairs, declared that 'in the recesses of the Seraglio Mahmud caught a light which never penetrated there before,' the light of Christianity."

"Historians recognize the fact that Mahmud was the only sultan of the Ottoman Dynasty in modern times who possessed the qualities of a great ruler."

The awesomeness of prayer. . . .

How They Prayed in Secret!

Nothing is more revolting than to witness the Pharisaical praying in public places of those who desire to be seen of men and counted pious. The motive in these cases would debar the presence of God from the act, for He will not share His glory with the pride of man.

But when accidentally someone has entered into the secret place of the one holding converse with Him Who inhabits Eternity, the result is awesome. It may be a very insignificant individual who is holding such secret converse with his God, but there is an unaccountable Presence!

"The sight of someone praying is wonderfully impressive," said a Salvation Army officer, Vander Werker. "When we have unawares seen a comrade who, thinking himself or herself alone, is in touch with God—why are we so affected? Why do we silently and quickly draw back? Surely we feel that there are two in that room; the one in contact with the Other. Holy is the place where our feet stand. Once, in mid-Celebes, just as we were going out in the darkness to the meeting place, I espied one of our Toradja soldiers, a lad of about sixteen, standing in the shadow of the house—praying: his dark, boyish face uplifted to the starry sky. I felt wonderfully strengthened by that boy's presence in the meeting, for here was one who had just been in contact with the Invisible."

Samuel Chadwick, whom God later used so mightily in His harvest field in England, muses about a hallowed scene that remained with him all his life.

"When I was a very small boy, not more than six or seven years of age, I was sent on an errand to the house of a neighbor named Davenport; it was about nine o'clock in the morning. I knocked, lifted the sneck, and stepped inside. On the hearth, kneeling at a chair on which was an open Bible, was Mrs. Davenport, praying. She was unaware of my presence. I stood in silent awe for a moment, and then quietly stepped out and closed the door. It is more than sixty years since that morning, but from then till now I have known that Mrs. Davenport was a saint of God, because she prayed. It is God's infallible sign, and it is the only sign that even the world accepts as an infallible proof."

· · · · ·

The cultured and wealthy Baron Watteville had come to the Moravian settlement at Hernhutt because he was interested in these settlers. Loving solitude and also the company of the common people, he had chosen to reside in one of their humble abodes rather than in the castle. He was awakened very early one morning by voices raised in the room adjoining. As the partition was very thin, the Baron could hear every word of these single-hearted Christians. Their prayer moved him deeply. His own heart was aflame, and he, too, began to pray with great fervor and importunity.

Finding the walls of the room almost closing him in, he went out of doors under the vault of heaven and walked in the timber yard of Christian David, a leader among the Moravians. There, he found a log and seating himself upon it began to review his entire life. He traced the providence of God which had led him to the same university as his friend, Count Zinzendorf.

His consecration to God was complete for all time—forever. Solemnly he dedicated himself to the service of God, the One Who had so graciously led his footsteps to this Moravian settlement. Time passed so quickly that he was unaware of what was going on around him, until he heard the words of the carpenter saying, "There, at last it is done, and we shall be able to lay the first stone of the new house today."

"And I also," joined in the Baron. "I am ready, and I will help you."

That evening when the stone was laid, the Baron placed underneath it his rings and jewelry and all that spoke of his old life—everything that would bind him to his old life.

After the dedication talk by Count Zinzendorf, the Baron kneeled down on the stone and poured forth such a fervent, Spirit-filled prayer as he gave himself unreservedly to the service of Christ that all who heard were in tears. Zinzendorf himself said he had never witnessed such a passioned prayer, and he attributed the mighty movement of God that was set in motion very soon afterwards to that scene.

The awesomeness of prayer! How little we know how it might affect the most worldly-minded listener.

The prayers those humble Moravians prayed that early morning had not been meant for the ears of man, but God honored their petitions. The awesomeness of that prayer produced results which would reach the farthest shores of the habitable world. They also helped to secure to Count Zinzendorf a fully consecrated helper who proved to be what Melancthon had been to Luther.

•　•　•　•　•

Two godless young men in Ohio heard that an elderly Christian woman frequently went into the old, dilapidated log church by herself. Determined to discover the reason, they hid in the loft to await her unusual visit.

J. B. Finley, in *Sketches of Western Methodism,* graphically relates the story of the lone intercessor and what issued as a result of those private interviews with God.

"At an early day, in the settlement of that part of the country, a small Methodist society was organized by pioneer Methodist preachers. After some time, the society built that log church and flourished for several years. In the progress of time, however, some of the old members died and were buried in the graveyard close by the sanctuary, and others moved away, till it was dropped from the list of appointments as a preaching place, and only one member of the class and society remained.

"She was a 'mother in Israel' and, like the prophet, she was left to sigh over the desolations of Zion. She loved the old sanctuary and, though it was deserted, she seemed to realize an increasing attachment as time wrought its inroads upon its doors and windows.

"Invariably on the Sabbath, when her health and the weather would permit, did she repair to this deserted temple and worship her God. There, in holy meditation, did she recall the scenes of her youth, the holy seasons, happy days she had spent with her brethren and sisters, some of whom were sleeping quietly in the adjoining churchyard, while others were far away. Here she would sit, and read, and sing, and pray, and talk to her invisible God and Saviour.

"At length it was noised abroad that she was a witch, that the old church was haunted with evil spirits, and that she met there to hold communion with the spirits of darkness, and thus increase her power of evil over the bodies and souls of those around her. She was old and feeble, and heard their surmises; but she remembered that her Master was charged with being possessed by the devil. And she heeded them not, but continued her Sabbath visits to the consecrated place.

"Two wicked young men of the neighborhood determined to watch her and, entering the church some time before she arrived, they climbed up and secreted themselves in the clapboard loft. After remaining there a short time they saw the old lady enter the church and take her seat by the rude altar.

"The young men, as they afterward related, experienced some sensations of fear, seeing, as they supposed, the old witch draw from her side pocket an old leather enveloped book. But their fears soon subsided when they heard her read, instead of an invocation to the spirits of darkness, the story of the widow of Sarepta. After she had finished, she drew from her other pocket an antiquated looking hymnbook, from which she read that inimitable hymn—

'Jesus, I my cross have taken,
All to leave and follow Thee;
Naked, poor, despised, forsaken,
Thou from hence my all shalt be.'

"After having sung this beautiful hymn, which she did with a trembling, but sweet, melodious voice, she fell on her knees and poured out her full heart to God in prayer and supplication. As friend holds fellowship with friend, so did she talk with her heavenly Father. She told the Lord all her complaints and grievances, and lamented the sad condition of the old and young of the neighborhood, who were alike on the road to perdition.

"She then alluded to the happy seasons she had enjoyed in the place, when Zion shed her holy light, and converts crowded her gates. In piteous strains she lamented her desolations, and prayed that the Lord would build up her waste places and again crowd her gates with living converts. She prayed especially for those who cast out her name as evil, that the Lord would change their hearts. She prayed also for the young and giddy multitude who were forgetting God and living as if there were no hell to shun, no Heaven to pursue.

"While she was praying, God's Spirit was at work on the hearts of the young men in the loft, and they began to weep and cry for mercy. The old lady was not startled. She seemed to realize, while praying, an answer to her prayer. And as the Saviour invited Zacchaeus to come down from the tree, because on that day salvation had come to his house, so did she invite those young men to come down from their hiding place. They obeyed her directions, and there at that altar, where, in other days, she had witnessed many conversions, before the Sabbath sun sank behind the western hills, they found pardon and salvation.

"From this hour the work of God commenced. The meetings were continued, and a flourishing church was raised up. And the old dilapidated log meeting house was again made to resound with the happy voices of the children of Zion."

• • • • •

J. R. Miller, in his book, *Come Ye Apart*, tells how at sixteen he carelessly opened the door of his mother's room, not knowing she was engaged in her devotions. "There he saw her bowed in prayer, pleading so earnestly with God that she had not been disturbed by his entrance. Instantly he withdrew, awed by the solemnity that filled the place; but as he softly closed the door, he heard his own name, and the fragment of a sentence of prayer which revealed to him the fact that his mother was making intercession for her boy. Through all the events of the crowded years since, that day has been a power both of restraint and inspiration in the writer's life. In times of temptation, far from home, that holy picture has shone out in the darkness. . . . It is utterly impossible to measure the influence on the writer's life of that one moment's glimpse of his mother on her knees. It was a revelation and told not only of one prayer that particular day, but of like intercession every day and every night."

J. R. Miller said, "It is very precious comfort even to know that a dear human friend is praying for us. Many a time in my youth was I kept from doing wrong things by the thought that in the quiet home far away my father and my mother, every morning and every evening, stretched out holy hands in earnest, loving prayer that God would keep their boy. I could not do the wrong thing with this vision in my mind. Still more powerful in its restraining influence upon us should be the assurance that day and night Jesus in Heaven is thinking of us, watching us from His holy height in glory, and at every appearance of evil prays for us. How could we do the evil thing if we but stopped long enough to think of this divine intercession for us?"

Prayer has been defined as "Love on its knees." He who loves God will seek to be often in His presence, cultivating the One Who is love. He who is assured of that ineffable love will never feel an orphan in an alien world.

•   •   •   •   •

Dr. George Truett in a magazine article told of the power of his own mother's prayers over his life when but a child. "May I speak a word about my mother, now in that yonder land these last few years, the best Christian I ever saw? May I speak a word about her faith?

"I was reared in a large family, far out on the farm, and I remember that when Father and the older boys used to go to the farm, the least little fellow, about four, and myself, about six, too little to work, stayed behind, and many are the times I have seen my mother in the morning sobbing, and I have gone and said: 'Mother, what makes you cry?' And she would say, 'You are too little, my boy, to understand. Never mind. Don't worry about Mother.'

"And when the breakfast was over and all the little things were done about the house in the morning, Mother has said to the two little boys: 'Now, you stay here while Mother goes aside to be alone a little while.' And she would go away with face suffused with tears, and she would come back in a little while, and every time she would come back singing, with a smile on her face fairer than the morning.

"And one morning I said to the little brother: 'What do you guess happens to Mother? She goes away crying, and she comes back singing. Let us see what it is.' We followed along quietly behind her, and she went there into the orchard near the little country home, and we saw her and heard her. She was down on her face before God. I can remember until yet the surpassing pathos of her prayers.

"She said, 'Lord Jesus, I never can rear this houseful of boys like they ought to be reared, without Thy help. I will make shipwreck with them, without Thy help. I cannot guide them. I cannot counsel them. I cannot be the mother that a woman ought to be to her children, without God's help. I will cleave to Thee. Teach me and help me every hour.' I heard her like that, and then she came back, singing, every morning.

"And when I grew older, and when manhood was reached, and when I learned in my heart what it is to know Jesus, I knew the secret into which my mother entered. She was the greatest

Christian I ever saw. It is when you and I tread the path of secret prayer that we find out about Jesus, and are given to enter into the secret of His presence.

· · · · ·

Listen, too, to what Rev. Lionel B. Fletcher has to say on this subject of the awesomeness of prayer: "A publican, who was a drunkard, was converted under my ministry in New Zealand. He had lost his job, for brewers have not much sympathy with drinking when they have to pay for the beer drunk. He came to me after he was converted, and said, 'I can't preach; I can't even pray in public, but I could keep the Lord's house sweet and clean. Let me have the job of caretaker.' We gave it to him, and one day, when I found him on his knees dusting, I said, 'I'll show you how to polish up the bright work, George. I learnt how when I was a sailor.' And I showed him how to dust and polish without needing to go down on his knees. Then he said, 'You don't understand. I polish the pew kneeling, and as I do it I pray, "Lord, whoever sits in this pew next Sunday, let them get the same blessing I got." '

"I came into the church one day, and I heard a voice. I had my key, and the caretaker had his key, but no one else had one. I wondered if thieves had got in, as they had been doing in some churches not long before. I crept up the back stairs to my pulpit, and there I saw George, with his hands stretched out before him and his face shining. He was praying for me, with voice choking because of his intensity. I got behind him, and heard him say, 'Lord, when he stands here on Sunday, let him bring the people to Jesus Christ, as he brought me.' He seemed filled with the Holy Ghost as he prayed that the Lord would fill me; and the next Sunday the service was swept by revival. As he saw people coming up to the front and taking my hand, the man who once was a publican, a drunkard, and an outcast, perfumed the church with power."

· · · · ·

The atmosphere of prayer is indeed awesome, because the place of prayer is the communication point between two realms, earth and Heaven. As the above examples have shown, the effects of prayer upon a silent observer or listener can be very powerful and far-reaching. The following little story provides a further illustration of this truth, and is taken from a very old magazine.

"I was invited to aid a pastor in Delaware County, Pennsylvania, during a revival about eleven years ago. A young man, now a missionary in New York, also assisted in the meetings for prayer. When I was about to leave, I was accompanied on my way for a mile or more by the pastor and the young man. We parted at a spot surrounded on three sides by woods; from the open side a field could be seen at some distance on a hill. Full of solemn feeling, we could not part without prayer. An old treetop lay before us, and one of the company proposed to kneel down among its branches, not wishing any but the all-seeing Eye to rest upon us. All three prayed. We parted.

"Three months afterward, a letter from the pastor informed me that among the persons received into his church, the fruits of the revival, was one who traced his first serious impressions, which resulted in his conversion, to the scene above described. While ploughing on the hillside, he had seen three men bow together in prayer in the fallen treetop, and the *sight* of prayer had so affected him, that he could find no peace until he became himself a praying man.

"Thus is 'praying in secret' rewarded openly. Thus varied are the ways in which the Holy Spirit carries conviction to the conscience. Were Christians more frequently found on their knees, in their closets, in parting hours, and in social gatherings, there would be more converts to trace their religious impressions to the sight and hearing of prayer."

She couldn't resist his entreaties. . . .

How a Son Prayed for His Mother

The awesomeness of prayer is shown once again in the following incident told in the book *Footprints of an Itinerant.* In the Gaddis home, word had been received that their son, John, had joined the Methodists, which in those days was highly offensive news. The father set out to the scene of the outdoor services that he might order his son to return home.

Mr. Gaddis found his son and immediately inquired if he had become a member of that despised sect, and upon hearing his answer in the affirmative, he was highly displeased. But his displeasure gave way to wrath when he understood his son had gotten saved. He was sorry for the day he had ever been born, and ordered the young man to precede him at the point of his cane. On the journey homeward, however, the father had time for more reflection, and fearing lest he might be fighting against God, he determined on a less severe measure. John's brother, who later became the itinerant, now takes up the story.

"Things continued in this state, with but little variation, for about two weeks. But the time of deliverance was near at hand. God unexpectedly wrought out for His servant a glorious victory. A Methodist prayer meeting was appointed at the house of Mr. Maffitt, who resided in the immediate vicinity of my father's residence. As soon as my brother heard of it, he manifested a great desire to attend. He made known his wishes first to my father, who tried in vain to persuade him not to attend. Finding all arguments of no avail, he at last consented, provided it met the approbation of my mother. But when the subject was mentioned to her, she became much displeased, and told him plainly she never would consent to his going among the Methodists again. He pled with her to change her purpose, but it was all in vain. She at last told him if he did go to that prayer meeting contrary to her wishes, she would immediately follow him and bring him home. She also said that she felt it to be her duty, as a parent, if possible, to restrain him from bringing any additional obloquy upon the family—she would COMPEL him to obey her commands at all hazards.

"The crisis had now arrived, and the 'enemy came in like a flood.' The faith of my brother seemed to falter, but he retired for prayer, and soon the Spirit came to his aid and stilled the voice of the 'accuser.' Satan, earth, and hell were all doomed to a speedy discomfiture. As the shades of evening drew nigh, my brother remembered the words of St. Paul, 'In every thing by prayer and supplication let your requests be made known unto God.' He retired to the barn for secret prayer, confidently believing that God would make the path of duty plain. He 'continued in prayer,' knowing that 'vain is the help of man.' As the shades of night gathered around, he was still alone upon his knees, 'wrestling with the angel of the covenant,' resolved not to give over the struggle till he should 'prevail with God and man.'

"After Mother had arranged her domestic affairs for the evening, she looked around for my brother, but could not find him about the house. She at once concluded that he had gone to the prayer meeting, notwithstanding she had forbidden him in the most positive manner. She instantly resolved to follow him and oblige him to return. She hastily put on her sunbonnet and left the house in a great rage, breathing out terrible threatenings against the Methodists and all who attended their meetings. But here let us notice the remarkable interposition of divine Providence. God had no doubt been guiding and overruling this whole affair.

"The path leading to Mr. Maffitt's passed near the barn, and as Mother approached it she heard the earnest but plaintive voice of someone at prayer. She paused and listened for a while, and finally concluded to leave the path and go around to the rear of the building, where she could listen unobserved to the prayer of the unknown suppliant. But imagine her astonishment! When she had reached the most favorable position for the accomplishment of her wishes, she recognized the voice of her own son! At that moment he was pleading in strong faith with God to open the 'eyes of the understanding' of his mother; that being enlightened she might 'know what is the hope of his calling, and what the riches of the glory of his inheritance in the saints.' The cries and words which he uttered were sharper than a two-edged sword. She was powerfully convicted by the Spirit of God, and instantly convinced of the depravity of her heart and the wickedness of her conduct toward her dear child who was so faithfully trying to save his own soul. She was seized with trembling; her whole frame shook, and her strength left her in a moment. She had to take hold of the logs of the old barn to keep from falling to the earth. She concluded that she occupied 'enchanted ground,' and that her only safety was in flight. She determined to make a pre-cipitate retreat from the scene of conflict. But her strength was inadequate to the undertaking. It was with great difficulty that she kept from falling at every step. She felt afraid the earth would open and swallow her up before she could reach her home.

"On arriving at the house her strength was almost entirely exhausted. She soon rallied, and engaged in arranging her domestic affairs for the night, but when she reflected on her con-duct during the day, her soul was overwhelmed with a sense of guilt and shame. 'What have I been doing? Persecuting my inno-cent child! O, will God pardon? Will He ever forgive me? I am worse than Saul of Tarsus. He acted ignorantly when engaged in persecuting the people of God, but I am without excuse. I knew I was doing wrong. But family pride urged me forward. I abhor myself, and repent in dust and ashes.'

"My brother returned to the house not long afterward, and soon retired to bed, entirely ignorant of what had transpired. He felt, however, that his prayers were heard, and that he had better not go to the prayer meeting on that evening. God also assured his heart, 'that enlargement and deliverance' would come from another place. He felt that he had done his duty, and all that now remained was to continue to wait on the Lord, or stand still and see His salvation. After committing himself to the care of a covenant-keeping God, he was soon locked in the embrace of sleep.

"But in another part of that same dwelling there was one heart not at rest, one from whose eyelids sleep had departed. Father was asleep, but Mother could find no rest for her wounded soul. The arrows of 'the Almighty were drinking up her spirits.' She was now subdued into penitence at the feet of her offended Lord and Master. The pride of her heart was brought down, and humbled under the mighty hand of God. It might now be said of her as of one of old, 'Behold she prayeth!' and the burden of that cry was, 'Lord, save me or I perish.' 'God be merciful to me a sinner.'

"My father had fallen into a profound sleep, and all was quiet and silent as the grave. However, the agony of my mother soon became so great that she 'cried out in the night watches upon her bed.' This aroused my father, and spread alarm through all that part of the house. Father sprang out on the floor, lighted a candle, and went to the bed and cried out, 'Mary! Mary! Mary! do tell me what is the matter with you!' My mother made him no reply, but with her hands clasped upon her breast, with streaming eyes, continued, in the most plaintive manner, to plead with God, for Christ's sake, to have mercy upon her soul. Her constant cry was:

'Merciful God, Thyself proclaim,
    In this polluted breast;
Mercy is Thy distinguished name,
    And suits the sinner best.'

"My father was alarmed and bewildered. He ran into the other part of the dwelling and awoke my brother John, and said, 'Come, O come quickly into my room; your mother has an attack of the "hysterics." Come, get up, and go for the doctor. I fear she will die soon unless she gets relief.' John arose and concluded to go and see his mother before he started for the physician. On entering her bedroom, he soon discovered that she had no need of medical assistance. He knew that she had been wounded by the 'Spirit's sword,' and could only be healed by an application of 'Gilead's balm.' Christ, the Physician of the sin-sick soul, was all she wanted now. As soon as Mother discovered my brother at her bedside, she entreated his forgiveness, and asked him to get down and pray to God to forgive her also, and change her nature, too. My brother instantly fell upon his knees, and cried to God to set her soul at liberty, and to make her also a 'partaker of like precious faith with himself.' O, it was a time of deep anguish! The conflict lasted for several hours. But, like the Syrophenician woman, she continued to cry, 'Lord, help me.' At last the Comforter came, and said to the 'weeping Mary,' 'Daughter, be good cheer; thy sins, which were many, are all forgiven thee: go in peace and sin no more.' It was in that hour

'Her tongue broke forth in unknown strains
And sang redeeming love.'

"My mother shouted aloud for joy, and my brother rejoiced with her. The balance of the night was nearly all spent in prayer and praise. My father, who had been an eyewitness of all that passed, said the only thing that comforted him at the time was the reflection that it had all occurred in the night—the neighbors would not know it, and the family would be saved from disgrace. I have often heard him state he thought they were both partially deranged, and would be restored to their senses by the light of the morning. This, however, was a delusive hope.

"After the conversion of my mother, she ceased to oppose my brother in trying to secure a 'crown of life.' In regard to their religious experience, they now saw 'eye to eye,' and walked together from day to day in the comforts of the Holy Ghost.

"It was not long till my father was better reconciled to the unexpected change in my mother's experience; but the time was drawing near when he was to be subjected to a more severe trial than anything that had yet transpired.

"The following morning Father assembled the family, as usual, for worship. He read a Psalm, and then sung it, and kneeled down to pray; but soon after he commenced Mother began to praise God in an audible voice. This was a breach of decorum my father could not endure. He ceased praying at once, rose up from his knees, and left the house. He did not return again till called in to breakfast. This was of frequent occurrence during the week.

"On the following Sabbath the family, as usual, went to their own church. Mother, as yet, had never thought of going to the Methodist meetings, although she had resolved to cease persecuting her son, or any that wished to join them, in future. The services were unusually solemn on that day. The sacrament of the Lord's supper was administered. The 'preparation sermon' was on the sufferings of Christ. Mother, although a member of the Seceder church from a child, had never experienced a change of heart till a few days previous. Now everything was changed, because she had a 'new heart and a right spirit.' The Bible was a new book; its promises were precious; and the preaching of the Gospel was 'like honey from the comb' to her spiritual appetite. She was no longer an 'outer-court' worshiper, serving God in the 'letter.'

"The sermon was well adapted to the occasion, and long before its close my mother was very happy. The Lord poured into her soul the fullness of the riches of His grace—'good measure, pressed down, shaken together, and running over.' She shouted aloud for joy. The consternation of both minister and people was very great, as Mother continued to 'bless God in His sanctuary.' At length, the minister was overwhelmed with confusion, and took his seat in the pulpit; a part of the congregation fled from their seats toward the door, with great fear and trembling; the services were speedily brought to a close, and as the congregation returned home, they said one to another, 'We have seen strange things today.'

"Among all of them that retired from the house that day, none were so deeply chagrined as my father. His deep sense of mortification could only be exceeded by the joy and happiness of my mother and brother John. Such an occurrence had never been witnessed in that church before, and of course the members, as well as the preacher, were loud in their expression of condemnation. Mother was considered, by all of them, partially deranged, and, if not restored, would soon be a fit subject for the insane asylum."

The second Sunday the church was fuller than usual. New faces were seen among the audience as rumors had spread throughout the district about the strange happenings in the Seceders' church. All went quite smoothly until about half way through the sermon, when joyous hallelujahs poured from the converted mother. The minister sat down waiting for the noise to subside, but Mrs. Gaddis went on for some time before she ceased her praising. The son's report tells of the reaction. "The audience seemed overwhelmed with the sense of the majesty and power of God. I have heard my father remark that he would have given all he possessed to be free from the odium thus brought upon the family. . . . He was well persuaded that, whenever the Spirit filled her heart, whether at home or abroad, she would 'do as the occasion served.'"

On the third Sunday, the congregation had again increased, as more had come to see for themselves. When, however, Mrs. Gaddis began praising this time, the minister loudly called out for "Order! Order! Order." Finding that the joyful convert did not heed his imperative command, he asked the elders to put the woman out. No elder, however, rose to obey the pastor's command, and in the meantime Mrs. Gaddis continued to praise God until all were melted to tears. When the shouting ceased, the minister hastily dismissed the service, and the congregation left, some weeping and others murmuring.

The Methodists in the neighborhood were highly delighted, but the minister of the Seceders was incensed. Mrs. Gaddis' husband went home skeptical about when the whole thing would end.

Early in the week the noisy convert received a notification that she was to appear before the session charged with disorderly conduct— "shouting three successive Sabbaths." Mrs. Gaddis was indeed in a dilemma. She did not wish to be put out of the church of her early choice. She cried much but went to prayer as her source of comfort, and her prayers were not in vain. When they arrived at the session they were all awaiting the entrance of the accused. Mr. Gaddis was met by the committee and invited to a private session, and here he was asked to give the story of all that had transpired. "You all know I do not believe in shouting," he replied, "but I am compelled to state that my wife is a changed woman. She is not like the same person that she was once. She is kind, patient, and forbearing and seems to be happy all the time at home. . . . Sometimes she goes to secret prayer, and comes out of her closet bathed in tears. . . . She says she does not wish to shout, but, when 'filled with the Spirit,' she cannot and does not wish to refrain from so doing. I want you to call her in and let her answer for herself."

Upon asking the husband whether he had not tried to use his authority with her in asking her to desist, the husband said he had but it made no difference. The conference was ended.

The session, after a time of consultation, asked for the husband to return and said, "Mr. Gaddis, on more mature deliberation we have concluded not to examine Mrs. Gaddlis upon the charge preferred against her, or to inquire any further, at present, into the peculiar nature of her religious exercises. We also have unshaken confidence in her piety and integrity, and do not wish to throw any obstacles in her way. . . . We will dismiss the case, with the request that you will use all your influence to get her to quit shouting in church." The husband promised that he would.

Mrs. Gaddis could not refrain from praising God on the road home. These weeks were the happiest weeks in her whole life. Soon she attended a class meeting in the Methodist church with John. There she felt they understood her praises, and soon she was attending regularly with her son whom she had previously opposed so vehemently.

When desire becomes prayer. . . .

How a Mother Prayed for Her Son

I have a boy to bring up. . . .

What a priceless legacy Thou hast given me, O God, an eternal soul to shape and mold, to train and instruct. I am his constant companion, so he will look to me as a model of what a Christian should be. Keep me pure and holy by the precious blood of Jesus. May there be no discrepancy between what I am and what I profess to be.

I have a boy to bring up. . . .

Partner me in this most difficult task. I am inadequate, therefore I need to draw from Thine infinite resources through unceasing prayer and reading of Thy Word. My supplies of patience are scanty; Thine are inexhaustible. When the kettle boils over, the clothes line breaks, when visitors unexpectedly arrive on my scene of chaos—in fact when everything seems to go wrong then give me Thy calm. When I see wrong influences begin to dull his childish faith in Thee, then may I pray. May he long remember a mother's prayers.

I have a boy to bring up. . . .

Help me to never spurn that plaintive plea, "Spend time with me, Mummy." Though it puts me to great inconvenience, give me patience to let him work with me even if it takes twice as long to finish the task. Let him feel that he is sharing in the daily duties of life and learning the joy of creating. May I never become so over-occupied with the needs of others that I neglect this precious charge of mine. May he never grow up soured with religion, because he is left with baby-sitters every evening while I go out to engage in Christian activities. However, may he understand my need for Christian fellowship and be willing to experience some sacrifice when I find it necessary to leave him for a few evenings in order to enjoy such fellowship.

I have a boy to bring up. . . .

You know, dear Lord, the degree I might have had, that French course I would love to have taken, those books I might have read, only You asked me to take on the education of my boy rather than put him, in these formative years, into the hands of worldly-wise teachers. Only You know just what it has cost, and yet, I thank You for the deepening bonds between my boy and me, for the joy of sharing in the process of learning together, of being able to ensure that nothing contrary to Thy dear Word is being foisted upon his impressionable mind. I know he will eventually have to face the world alone, but may I seize these precious, early years and prayerfully fill them with principles and standards he shall never forget.

I have a boy to bring up. . . .

Help me, and in this particularly I need divine grace and strength, to instill in him the principle of obedience to higher authority. May I never tire of the endless task of bending his will to mine only in order that it may be easier for him to yield his will to his Heavenly Father. May I never by worldly compromise fail my boy in this unpopular task of discipline.

I have a boy to bring up. . . .

Dear Lord, may I put it on record that my wish for this child You have given into my care is that he be God's man. That the work of salvation which You have begun in his childish heart may grow and develop. I can only do so much; Thou must do the rest! I can train him. Thou canst change him! I can curb him. Thou canst transform him! I can influence him. Thou canst possess him! Then, give me strength, courage, determination, that I MAY BRING HIM UP FOR THEE.—Trudy Tait.

God's Masterpiece

She was leaving our city—this friend of mine, a grand-mother much older than myself, and I was visiting her for the last time before her departure. I would miss her sage wisdom and kind advice.

Back and forth along the years we went, intermingling the past and present, and seasoning the whole with hopes and plans for the future. We spoke of her new home. We spoke of my children, their music, their health. We spoke of these busy days, so full that oftentimes one's strength failed in the doing. For myself I expressed a burning desire for time to read, for time to write, but always there were too many things that had to be done. Her answer came as a blessing.

"My dear," she said, "you have in your care the Masterpiece of God. The greatest bit of writing that you could door that any-one has ever done—cannot compare with one child. The greatest paintings fade to nothing, the greatest pieces of sculpture fall to bits in comparison with God's Masterpiece—the child.

"Those children," she went on, "will take your very soul. They will take your energy, your whole being, and there will not be strength for the multitude of other things you want to do, but these are as nothing when you can work with the greatest thing in God's universe."

I was humbled and thankful for her words. I came home and bowed my head in meditation. I thought of the Master Who, when asked, "Who is the greatest in the Kingdom of Heaven?" had called a child and set him in the midst, and I knew that God's greatest blessing rests on those who minister to a little child.—Clelle L. Scot.

. . . . .

"It is said that there is enough electricity in one drop of water to generate two thunderstorms, so there are two latent antagonistic Eternities wrapped up in the heart of a little child."—D. Panton.

They were workers together with God. . . .

How Parents Prayed

Three persons were involved in this intricate pattern of prayer. There was a father in Aberdeen deeply concerned about his daughter; there was his daughter, a stranger on a trip to Edinburgh, also praying; and there was a Christian young woman in Edinburgh who obeyed the inward urge to speak to a perfect stranger. How different might have been the story had the father not prayed, and had the servant of Christ not been obedient to that inward prompting of the Spirit.

The Christian, a paper printed in London, many years ago told the story on the authority of Rev. J. H. Wilson of Edinburgh.

"A Christian girl in Edinburgh observed on the street a young lady—in charge of some children—who seemed sad. She ventured to ask the nursemaid whether she was a Christian.

" 'Who bade you ask that?'

" 'The Lord bade me,' was the reply.

" 'The Lord? I have been praying that if there is a God in Heaven, He would send someone to speak to me about my soul.'

"The young lady then explained that she was from Aberdeen, had accompanied her mistress to Edinburgh on a visit, and had been deeply impressed by a sermon she had heard from the lips of Dr. Bonar.

"Maggie—the zealous young Christian who had accosted the stranger—was not very competent to instruct a sinner in the way of salvation. But she did, at parting, quote these words of Jesus: 'Him that cometh to me I will in no wise cast out.'

"Two days later the stranger found Maggie and announced that she had found Jesus. And not long afterward she came again—this time bringing her sister. The three had a little prayer meeting together, and the sister went away rejoicing in the hope of salvation."

And what lay back of all this? A father's prayers! For Maggie soon received this letter:

"Dear Miss M____:

"You will, perhaps, think me rather forward in writing to you, but I feel as if my heart would burst with gratitude for the kindness you have shown to my daughters in being the means of leading them to the Saviour. I have long prayed for them both, and when they left here to go to Edinburgh, I prayed that the good Lord would save them both before they came back. He has heard my prayer.

"On the same day that you spoke to Mary, I was ill in bed. And as I prayed for my daughters, I felt the preciousness of the text, 'Him that cometh to me I will in no wise cast out.'

"You can, perhaps, fancy my joy when by the next post came a letter to tell me that Mary had found Jesus from that very text. Dear Miss M____, I cannot thank you enough, but the Lord will reward you for the joy you have brought to an old father's heart. You will excuse the writing; I am well-nigh seventy years old.

"I have only one thing to ask you; if you get a holiday in the summer, come and see poor old David; you will be made as welcome as the angels in Heaven. Mary says you are an orphan, but you will never want a friend, lass, as long as Davie Ferguson breathes the breath of life. And at the Judgment you can take my Mary and Jane up to Jesus and say, 'Here are two that, by the Spirit's help, I led to Thee.' We all send our greatest love to you."

In this instance, a hidden cause—known only to God—lay back of those events which were exposed to human view. A sick father's earnest prayer was ascending in Aberdeen while the daughter was being reached savingly in Edinburgh.

•   •   •   •   •

Rev. C. B. Crane, pastor of the South Baptist Church of Hartford, Connecticut, wrote William Patton the following interesting account of the answer given to his father's prayers and faith:

"In the spring of 1835 I entered Hamilton College, New York, full of worldly ambition but a stranger to the grace of God. On a certain Sunday near the end of the term, though there was no special religious interest in the college, I was impressed so profoundly by the love of Christ for sinners that I at once devoted myself to His service. I promised not only to be His disciple, but also to give myself to the ministry of His Word.

"Yet I had entered Hamilton College solely for the purpose that, under Theodore Dwight, then at the head of its law school, I might qualify myself for the legal profession. And it was to me the wonder of wonders that I could so readily surrender what had been the purpose of my life and consecrate myself to a work which I had well-nigh abhorred.

"In thus readily changing the plan of my life, I was conscious of no struggle. I was borne onward as a vessel is impelled by the tide.

"My father, a calm, well-balanced, and thoughtful man, was then pastor of the church in the neighboring village of Cassville. I wrote him a letter announcing my purpose to live the Christian life and to enter upon the Christian ministry; also, I expressed my desire to unite myself with his church on a baptismal profession of my faith. In his reply, to my astonishment, he expressed no surprise at all.

"As he afterward related to me, a day or two before the eventful Sunday above mentioned, as he was riding alone in the round of his pastoral calls, his whole soul was drawn out in prayer to God that I might become a Christian man and a Christian minister. As he prayed, his desire rose to almost an agony of earnestness; when suddenly he gained the assurance that his prayer was granted. And he awaited my next letter in confident expectation that its contents would be what they were.

"Here is a case which, I am sure, will allow no rationalistic explanation. The 'nervous excitement' theory of revivals and conversion is not apposite. One man, so little given to fanaticism as to be almost cold-blooded, is praying, at a distance, for another man of a like disposition. And the second man, in a college where the state of religion is unusually unpromising, obtains an experience which is the exact answer to the prayer."

William Patton, in a book written on prayer, included the well-known story of the mother of Augustine and her indefatigable and unremitting prayer for her wayward son. Very few mothers have shown such perseverance at the Throne of Grace as did this godly woman as she pursued her son from city to city. She was amply repaid as is related below.

"Augustine grew up in Carthage, a young man of genius, of strong passions which led him into sensual excesses, and of intellectual pride which carried him into the heresy of the Manichaeans.

"His mother Monica, a pious Christian, mourned with deepest grief over the sins and errors of her gifted son and ceased not to pray for his conversion day and night. Augustine affectingly speaks of this in his penitential *Confessions*.

"'Thou sentest Thy hand from above and drewest my soul out of the profound darkness; my mother, Thy faithful one, weeping to Thee for me more than mothers weep for the bodily deaths of their children. For she, by that faith and spirit which she had from Thee, discerned the death wherein I lay, and Thou heardest her, O Lord; Thou heardest her and didst not despise her tears, which, streaming down, watered the ground under her eyes in every place where she prayed. Yea, Thou heardest her; for whence was that dream whereby Thou comfortedst her?'

"The dream was a vision of her son, symbolically represented as coming to the same position of faith and life as herself. But her faith was subjected to long testing. 'Almost nine years passed in which I wallowed in the mire of that deep pit and the darkness of falsehood, oft essaying to rise, but dashed down the more grievously. All which time that chaste, godly, and sober widow (such as Thou lovest), now cheered with hope, yet no whit relaxing in her weeping and mourning, ceased not at all hours of her devotion to bewail my case unto Thee.'

"His mother besought a bishop to argue with him. But, seeing that he was too opinionated and puffed up to be won in that way, the bishop replied, 'Let him alone awhile; only pray God for him. He will of himself, by reading, find out what that error is and how great its impurity.'

"When Monica urged her point, he added, 'Go thy way, and God bless thee; for it is not possible that the son of these tears should perish.' Which answer, Augustine says, she took as if it had sounded from Heaven.

"But now came a fresh trial of her faith, and also an illustration of the unexpected ways in which God answers prayer. Augustine announced his intention to remove to Rome.

" 'So why I went hence and went thither, Thou knowest, O God, yet showedst it neither to me, nor to my mother who grievously bewailed my journey and followed me as far as the sea. . . . And yet refusing to return without me, I scarcely persuaded her to stay that night in a place hard by our ship, where was an oratory [a place of prayer] in memory of the blessed Cyprian.

" 'That night I privily departed, but she remained in weeping and prayer, with so many tears, but asking of Thee that Thou wouldest not suffer me to sail. . . . For she loved to have me with her, as all mothers do, but much more than most; and she knew not how great joy Thou wast about to work for her out of my absence.'

"At Rome he taught rhetoric and soon went on to Milan to practice the same profession. Here he came into personal friendship with the celebrated Ambrose, under whose preaching, after many internal struggles to overcome his evil habits, he was converted from the Manichaean error. He was with his friend Alypius at the time of the final decision, and they made it together.

" 'Then,' writes Augustine, 'we went in to my mother [she had followed him to Milan] and told her, relating in order how it took place. Then did she leap for joy and triumph, and bless Thee, Who art able to do more than we ask or think.'

"May it not well be said that Monica had travailed in birth for her son spiritually as well as physically? What mother may not draw encouragement from her example to pray with faith for the conversion of her children? And who can tell what honor God will put upon parental importunity and perseverance? Monica's prayers saved Augustine, and Augustine's influence on the Christian church has been scarcely second to that of any uninspired man. He impressed the minds of Luther, Melanchthon, Calvin, Knox, and other reformers more than did any other author.

"Many, who are content with a superficial piety and have no deep earnestness for the salvation of their children, cannot understand how it is that some parents have assured faith and put forth prevailing prayer. It is through the indwelling of the Holy Spirit in truly consecrated parents, by reason of which they realize the necessity of conversion, that they are filled with intense longings for the salvation of their children, and are enabled to plead with broad intelligence God's covenant and promises."

It took years to learn. . . .

How Prayer Could Change Me!

Since I was brought up in a home where prayers were said regularly and frequently, it may seem strange that it took me years to learn to pray. But that's the truth.

I do not remember a day in my parents' home when I did not hear my father and mother pray in our closely knit family group—and it was a group, seven girls and two boys! Our mother taught us, "Now I lay me down to sleep," and my father taught us, "Our Father which art in Heaven."

Each day opened and closed with family prayer. Each meal was started with a prayer of thanks. We were taught by both our mother and our father that whatever we needed we should ask God for in prayer. This included especially the times when we might be in trouble or discouraged.

As an old person now, I can remember the first serious question that arose in my mind about prayer. I was just a young child, and the disappointment that came to me then brought this question about. Our very busy parents had promised us that on the next day we would have a family picnic if it did not rain.

Now, to children in this day, a family picnic may not mean much, and with all the facilities we have today, rain might not interfere. But to me, that picnic would be an epoch in my young life. So we began to pray that God would give us sunshine the next day.

A heavy morning downpour of rain, easing off to a steady, day-long shower, washed out any outdoor picnic plans.

I was puzzled. Why? Why did God ignore the simple request of a child with great faith?

THAT EVENING the answer came. It was the night of mid-week prayer meeting, and a farmer, a member of our church, was there with grateful smiles as he testified how God had certainly answered his prayers for rain that day, for the crops were fairly burning up for lack of water and too much hot sunshine.

Though just a child, I seemed to catch this larger view of the situation, for I saw that God knows better than any of us what is really best as the answer to prayer.

The next important chapter of my prayer life was written when our family was experiencing some serious difficulties. My father prayed and asked God for some help that he felt must be given and must be given soon.

On the wall of my father's and mother's bedroom was the motto, "PRAYER CHANGES THINGS." As I heard him pray with increasing intensity for the desired help, I looked at that motto and wondered, Does prayer really change things?

The immediate trouble worked up to a definite crisis, and his prayers were not answered in the way for which he had prayed. He said nothing, but the next morning, after God had answered in His way, I noticed a black line had been drawn through the word "things" on that motto, and above it my father had printed the word "me." It now read, "Prayer changes me."

My childlike conception of prayer had been that of a long-distance telephone call to God's switchboard in Heaven, seeking an immediate, favorable reply.

BUT A SERIOUS experience came crashing into my life to cloud my view. I was graduated from high school, and was planning to enter college to prepare for a teaching career, when a sudden stroke took my godly father and left my mother with eight children younger than I.

Was this what I had been praying for? Was this God's way for me?

Suddenly my thoughts about prayer were thrown into hopeless confusion. I continued through the mechanical repetition of prayer words, but all too often they meant little more to me than if I had fastened them to a motorized prayer wheel and kept it going continually while I went groping around.

A widowed mother, eight sisters and brothers—what COULD I do? How could I keep the home together, much less think of going to college?

I had gone into the deep, deep woods that stood not far from my home. For days I had been fighting or trying to fight the emotional upset that was surely getting its hold on me.

"DEAR LORD," I prayed, "help me find the right answer to this great problem facing me. Help me to not ask WHY—but to trust. You know, dear God, I have come into this quiet wood to find the help I need. I don't know just the words to speak that might remove the fears within; I don't know how to think victoriously over this disturbing problem; in fact I do not know how to let go and let YOU. But I do know that YOU KNOW. PLEASE help me now."

As I stayed quietly on my knees for a few minutes with that wholesome therapy all about me, it seemed that God, in those moments, took complete charge of my helpless situation.

I knew right then that my problems were not too hard for my God to solve. And with the Psalmist, I said, "In thee, O Lord, do I put my trust: let me never be put to confusion" (Psalm 71:1).

Once again I found my father's God, Who changed me instead of things, because I prayed to Him for help. A great miracle came into my life; my original problem and difficulties did not seem to be so big after considering His greatness in helping me carry the load.

YEARS HAVE passed now; God is still real in my life; my all is dedicated to Him Who, in His great love and tender mercy, let "prayer change me" instead of "things."

It may take years to learn to pray, but we can learn—and in such a way as to make prayer a personal "radio" or "TV equipment" for our lives, so that we can tune in for God's plan and be willing to say, AMEN. "PRAYER CHANGES ME"—not "things."

—Katherine Bevis in *Herald of Holiness*

•　•　•　•　•

Ada Habershon was the youngest daughter of Rev. S. O. Habershon, born January 8, 1861 in London. She authored several books, and wrote the poem, "I Am a Prayer."

I AM A PRAYER

I am a prayer, O Lord, a constant prayer,
I cannot tell Thee all my wants in words;
I have no eloquence with which to plead,
But 'tis enough—I am myself a prayer.
Like beggar whose outstretched hand appeals,
Or fledgling in the nest with open beak,
My case to Thee is mutely eloquent;
And seeing me Thou seest all my need,
For Thou Who mad'st my frame can always read
The language of desire it ever speaks.

Thou art the Answer, Lord, Thyself alone!
For every need Thou art the rich supply,
Thou art the "Yea" to all God's promises,
The sure "Amen" to every one I claim.
"Is it for me?" my heart with longing cries,
One sight of Thee proclaims a gladsome "Yea";
"Oh, make it mine," the yearning stronger grows,
"Amen, it shall be so," and it is done;
And as each promise is to me made good
Thou, Lord, in me art freshly glorified.

'Tis at the mercy-seat that Heaven and earth
In presence of the blood, communion hold,
And at the Throne the prayer and Answer meet—
The Answer waits before the prayer begins,
For Thou art first at every trysting place.
My wants all spring to Thee and gladly rest.
I've found the reason why Thou canst bestow,
Exceedingly abundant, far above
What I can ask or even think! It is
Because Thou art the Answer—I the prayer.

I am an answered prayer, but still I plead,
For as each want is met new wants arise,
And every day I crave the Answer still.
My very being is a constant prayer,
Each member adding words of mute request.
These empty hands need filling from Thyself,
And ask for strength to do their work for Thee;
The feet would fain be guided in the way,
That they, with oil anointed, may speed on,
And run the race which Thou hast run before;

Mine eyes need Thine illuminating beams,
That they may see Thy footprints and Thy face,
And gaze upon the wonders of Thy Word;
Mine ears need opening to Thy still, small voice;
My lips need touching with the living coal;
My tongue enflaming with Thy wondrous love,
That it may speak with glowing words of Thee;
My mouth fresh filling with the heavenly food,
And satisfying with the latter rain;
My brow needs daily sealing with Thy peace;
My heart with every beat proclaims its need,
And every breath I take repeats the tale.

So would I fain for evermore abide
Within the secret place of the Most High,
Like empty vessel in the flowing stream
That thus the prayer may in the Answer dwell.

Things were happening at midnight. . . .

How They Obeyed the Impulse To Pray

"At midnight Paul and Silas prayed, . . . And suddenly . . . all the doors were opened, and every one's bands were loosed" (Acts 16:25, 26).

Miraculous deliverances have been related by missionaries when traveling abroad on business for their beloved Master. Prayer is so real and potent a force that the intercessor can actually be appraised of danger to Christian workers thousands of miles away. The eye of God is over the righteous. He neither slumbers nor sleeps and is aware of the dilemmas which confront the lone ambassador. He has his protection and his highest interest at heart.

Now, God could intervene without the medium of prayer on the part of another Christian, but He has not chosen so to do. If we could gather together all the information of those involved when a miraculous deliverance is wrought, we would find a praying figure who was first alerted by an insistent prompting of the Holy Spirit or angelic messengers.

Surely, the following incidents are only a few among multitudes of happenings which would prove effectually that prayer has ascended to God on behalf of souls in danger, and deliverance has come in answer to those petitions.

"A lady whose life has been revitalized by this experience, keeps a diary, and compares notes with the people she prays for. One entry reads:

" 'I was awakened from a deep sleep one night, aware of an urgent need to pray for two girls traveling in Central Asia.'

"Their object was to meet and encourage isolated believers, many of whom were without fellowship and the Word of God.

The lady had pledged to pray regularly and did so, but this was different. In her nearness to God she recognized His voice calling her to pray a specific prayer of deliverance, protection, and safety for her friends in a dangerous situation. The diary goes on.

" 'I prayed and in a small measure realized something of what seemed like "agonizing in prayer." Eventually I felt a release and freedom to settle down again and go to sleep, and did so thanking God for answered prayer.'

"Months later she found out what had happened on that eventful day. The girls traveling in Central Asia were crossing from one country to another. They had entered no-man's land, the uninhabited area between the two countries, and were driving in the dry, barren desert, towards the first police post in the next country. One of them remarked on the apparent lack of traffic on the road. Apart from two soldiers, who were not immediately seen, nobody was at the border. Getting out of the car, the two girls went into the small hut to hand in their passports for inspection and to ask for the road barrier to be lifted. The soldiers were in the hut lying on the floor resting. The smoky atmosphere was charged with an indescribable, disturbing influence. The soldiers began to talk to each other. One of the girls, understanding the gist of the conversation, immediately cried to God for help. Gesturing to her friend to pray, she listened on.

"No one else seemed to be traveling that way. It was a holy day and people from both countries considered it an inauspicious day for traveling. The soldiers continued talking, making their unrepeatable plans for their own indulgence, and planning the murder of the girls in order to hide any incriminating evidence. What a predicament! The girl who did not understand the language did not realize their imminent danger. The other girl suffered from mixed feelings of genuine human fear and assurance of God's faithfulness in any situation. What would God do now? How would He deliver us today? Who would be praying at home?

"The conversation stopped abruptly, and one of the men got up off the floor. Taking a passport he examined it, making an uncomplimentary, although amusing comment on the not too flattering photograph. The other soldier got up and examined the second passport. When the situation was getting unbearable, there was noise outside. In surprise the soldiers looked out of the hut. Their reaction gave new hope to the girls. An old rusty bus ground to a halt at the barrier. It was filled and overflowing with people hanging on to every available bit of metal. As the bus stopped they fell off, their arms, hands, and legs tired from hanging on. They swarmed towards the hut. The conversation between the soldiers was heated, 'Where did this bus come from? Why were they traveling today?' Angrily they went to investigate. The girls grabbed their passports from the table and went out of the hut. In the rush one girl left her handbag behind and had to return and retrieve it. They reached the car, and immediately the barrier was lifted and the two girls triumphantly went on their way.

"They never waited to see why the bus was there. It seemed a mystery. They had no recollection of passing any bus or vehicle. Yet there were no side roads or stopping places in no-man's land, and the bus could only travel slowly. However, this was no mystery. The arrival of the bus was timed carefully to coincide with the situation of the girls. Also the prayers of the old lady thousands of miles away had been timed by the greatest Timekeeper of all—Jesus Christ, to demonstrate the power of prayer and His miraculous protection of His followers today. It was perfect timing.

"Do you know anything of this kind of prayer? Take the challenge and allow God to revitalize and recommission your life for such active service for 'Jesus Christ, Who is the same yesterday, and TODAY and forever.' "

• • • • •

We now turn our attention to a second striking incident of timely night prayer for those facing dangers thousands of miles away from loved ones and home. This account involves a missionary couple whom we knew well and can vouch for the veracity of the story.

It was in the depth of night when the intercessor was awakened out of sleep with an unaccountable sense of urgency. It had to do with a missionary couple whom she knew to be at the time traveling through Central Africa. An urgency to pray pressed on her mind, and prayer was begun for those two faithful souls driving through jungle in that unsettled and sparsely populated country.

Soon she awakened her sleeping husband who ever was a partner with her in prayer, and confided to him her fears. Together they interceded for this couple's need at the Throne of God's grace. At last they obtained relief, and felt God had heard them. Writing later to their missionary friends, they related the date and hour of night in which the intercession had been made. It coincided exactly with a most unusual happening in their lives in Central Africa.

The two had set up camp for the night on the roadside in this country abounding with wild game. The villages were few and far between. The night air resounded with the sounds of Africa's insect and animal life, and the beat of distant native drums. The very vastness of the country and the distances between garages or police depots presents a real danger problem in Africa.

They had not long been settled for the night in their Volkswagen, when a car drove up and a plantation owner stopped, pleasantly asking them the purpose of their encampment. It is quite usual in Africa for travelers to stop and inquire if they find another car by the roadside in case there is dire need. Upon telling him that they were just camping for the night, he urged them to come to his plantation nearby where they would enjoy the amenities and comforts unknown in so cramped a vehicle. He also confided to them his great isolation and that he had not for some time even seen a white face.

The missionaries quickly packed up and followed their friend. Soon they were shown to their bedroom, and their luggage was deposited. Then the three settled down on the veranda to enjoy some conversation as evening advanced. The husband had reason to leave the wife for a few minutes, doubtless to procure something from their van, and while he was gone, the plantation owner with a look of passion on his face confided to the young wife that he had not been able to enjoy a woman's fellowship for a very long time. He hinted of intimacies. Although her husband soon returned to his seat on the porch, she could not find privacy to tell him of the threat which haunted her. What made matters even worse was that their host announced to them that his generator had refused to work, and they would have to spend the night without the usual lighting.

The husband was busily writing and never noticed the constant eyeing of his wife by the plantation owner who sat opposite. All the while she was trying to think of what she should do. They were both unacquainted with the language of the native helpers who were employed on the estate. She pictured her husband's life being threatened. Any crime would go undetected in their isolated position, far from any protection of the law. Few would know of their whereabouts. Finally to her relief she found a brief opportunity to convey to her husband the menacing threat of their host. Her husband acted quickly and decisively, taking his terrified wife to their Volkswagen and locking her in.

He then proceeded to inform their host that they would not be staying the night after all, and that he wished to take his luggage from the upper floor bedroom. Settlers in Africa must needs be deft with the pistol, and the wife expected any moment to hear the report of gunfire. But to their surprise the man meekly showed the way to the bedroom, making no protest as the husband gathered their belongings and hastily made for their car. They wasted no time in setting off, glad to be away regardless of what the night might hold for them.

How could the prayer partners thousands of miles away know of the dilemma of the two who had hazarded their lives for the cause of Christ? The Eye that never sleeps had known of their predicament and had alerted praying ones, giving them such a sense of urgency and also giving them to know for whom to pray. It will never be known what designs that man would have carried out but for intercession made for the couple at that exact hour of their need.

• • • • •

A third instance might be cited of the time when Rev. Seth Rees, in the United States, was prompted by the Spirit to pray for a fellow-minister over in India.

"On one occasion he was seized with a strong burden of prayer for his dear friend, Rev. Charles Stalker, Quaker evangelist, who was then in India. He laid his burden before the 'Father Who seeth in secret,' never resting until his soul had somehow caught the assurance that it was heard. Not until some time afterward did he learn that his prayer synchronized perfectly with a gravely critical hour in an illness which his distant friend was undergoing. Recovery quickly followed. Charles Stalker has expressed the conviction that on a second occasion of great danger to his life, Seth Rees's prayers prevailed in his behalf."

• • • • •

The Bible speaks of a ladder from Heaven to earth on which angels are ascending and descending. The angels are pictured in the Bible as those who minister to the heirs of salvation. To those who have been spiritually initiated into the mysteries of the Kingdom this coming and going of angelic hosts is no surprise. Christians are the subject of heavenly visitants intent on delivering us in our times of extremity. But how can the uninitiated come to that intimacy with God where they can intercede effectually? Not all Christians are as advanced in a prayer life as to be recipients of such heavenly intelligence. We quote something which might help those young in grace to know how they too might enter into this wondrous privilege of intercession.

"The power of intercession is a slow growth. A man's praying power is not an arbitrary thing; it is the result of long antecedent spiritual processes. If a man finds himself an effective intercessor with God, a prince having power with God to prevail, it is only because he has grown to great spiritual wisdom, unselfishness, and grace. The praying power of a man is no mere accident of his mood, no mere impulse of his necessity. It is the slow growth of spiritual character, the gradual development of a faith that has 'grown exceedingly,' the confidence which a long familiarity with God creates, the fervent sympathy and desire of a chastened unselfishness, the ripened spirituality and tenderness of a carefully cultured heart.

"You cannot be worldly, selfish, and lukewarm today, living feebly and unspiritually, caring little for others, realizing but little of vivid, joyous communion with God, and tomorrow, become suddenly a man of fervent, large-hearted, mighty prayer. Spiritual life, like other life, has its laws of growth and power. Spiritual weakness does not suddenly develop into strength. Self-seeking is not magically transformed into self-forgetful intercession. A prayer such as this is perhaps the very highest achievement, the supremest grace, the most perfect fruit of the spiritual life; altogether impossible, therefore, to a man whose spiritual life is feeble."—Henry Allon.

"Giants in prayer are discovered in public, but they are made in private."—Ferrier Hulme.

> Teach me to pray, O Lord,
> Teach me to pray.
> Thy gracious aid afford,
> Teach me to pray.
> Help me to pray aright,
> More by faith, less by sight;
> Lead me with heavenly light.
> Teach me to pray.

Something had happened to Mrs. Whittemore. . . .

How She Prayed All Night

"I shall never forget a scene I witnessed many years ago in Boston," said Dr. R. A. Torrey. "It was at the international Christian Workers' Convention which was held in the old Tremont Temple, seating thirty-five hundred people. It was my privilege to preside at the Convention. On a Saturday morning at eleven o'clock the Tremont Temple was packed to its utmost capacity, every inch of standing room where men and women were allowed to stand was taken, and multitudes outside still clamoring for admission.

"The audience was as fine in its quality as it was large in its numbers. As I looked back of me on the platform, it seemed as if every leading minister and clergyman not only of Boston but of New England was on that platform. As I looked down in front of me I saw seated there the leaders in not only the church life but in the social and commercial and political life of Boston and the surrounding country. I arose to announce the next speaker on the program; and my heart sank, for the next speaker was a woman. In those days I had a prejudice against any woman speaking in public under any circumstances. But this particular woman was a professing Christian, and a Presbyterian.

"She had been what we call a 'worldly Christian,' a dancing, card-playing, theatre-going, low-necked dress Christian. She had had, however, an experience of which I had not heard. One night, sitting in their beautiful home in New York City, for she was a woman of wealth, she turned to her husband as he sat reading the evening paper and said: 'Husband, I hear they are doing a good work down at Jerry McAuley's Mission, let us go down and help them.' He laid aside his paper and said: 'Well, let us go.' They put on their wraps and started for Jerry McAuley's Mission.

"When they got there they found the Mission Hall full and took seats back by the door. As they sat there and listened to one after another of those rescued men, they were filled with new interest, a new world seemed opening to them; and at last the woman turned to her husband and whispered: 'I guess they will have to help us instead of our helping them. They've got something we haven't.'

"And when the invitation was given out, this finely-dressed, cultured gentleman and his wife went forward and knelt down at the altar in the sawdust along with the drunken men and other outcasts of the waterfront, and they got real salvation.

"But of this I knew nothing. I only knew the type of woman she had been, and when I saw her name on the program my heart sank and I thought, 'What a waste of a magnificent opportunity. Here is this wonderful audience and only this woman to speak to them.' But I had no authority to change the program, my business was simply to announce it. And summoning all the courtesy I could command under the circumstances, I introduced this lady, and then sank into the Chairman's seat and buried my face in my hands and began to pray to God to save us from disaster.

"Some years afterward I was in the City of Atlanta, and one of the leading Christian workers of that city, who had been at the Boston Convention, came to me and said: 'I shall never forget how you introduced Mrs. Whittemore at the Boston Convention, and then dropped into your chair and covered your face with your hands as if you had done something you were ashamed of.'

"Well, I had. But as I said, I began to pray. In a little while I took my face out of my hands and began to watch as well as pray. Every one of those thirty-five hundred pairs of eyes were riveted on that little woman as she stood there and spoke.

"Soon I saw tears come into eyes that were unaccustomed to weeping, and I saw men and women taking out their handkerchiefs and at first trying to pretend they were not weeping, and then, throwing all disguise to the winds, I saw them bow their heads on the backs of the seats in front of them and sob as if their hearts would break. And before that wonderful address was over that whole audience was swept by the power of that woman's words, as the trees of our Western forests are sometimes swept by the cyclone.

"This was Saturday morning. The following Monday morning Dr. Broadbeck, at that time pastor of the leading Methodist Church in Boston, came to me and said with a choking voice, 'Brother Torrey, I could not open my mouth to speak to my own people in my own church yesterday morning without bursting into tears as I thought of that wonderful scene we witnessed here on Saturday morning.'

"When that wonderful address was over, some of us went to this woman and said to her: 'God has wonderfully used you this morning.'

" 'Oh,' she replied, 'would you like to know the secret of it? Last night as I thought of the great throng that would fill the Tremont Temple this morning, and of my own inexperience in public address, I spent the whole night on my face before God in prayer.'

"Oh, men and women, if we would spend more nights before God on our faces in prayer, there would be more days of power when we faced our congregations!"

Two unforgettable prayers of a lowly itinerant. . . .

How He Prayed for the Mule and the Bishop!

The effectiveness of prayer is very strikingly illustrated in the following story. The writer, J. R. Lamont, felt the awesomeness of a humble prayer for the sick mule, in the middle of the night, in an old fashioned kitchen. He also remembered a humble and contrite prayer for the bishop in the rural community church. Now read the story as it was told in *The Watchman Examiner.*

"My father was an austere and very religious man. He made his living, a meager one, by tilling the soil with much hard labor of himself and, indeed, of the whole family, plus the unwilling assistance of a pair of rather dilapidated old mules. But he organized a church among the more or less devout of his neighbors, and they met every Sunday in the small country schoolhouse a mile or two distant from our home. Father also attended and assisted at many other religious meetings at various points within the radius of an hour or two of old Fanny's jog. Fanny was the one mule that could be induced to draw our family carriage, **and she did so under considerable protest.**

"That carriage—an open, one-seated, high-slung affair—was a character in itself. It was one of a kind. Its iron tires were induced to stay on the wheels by many windings of fence wire. Often in dry weather the creaking wheels were soaked overnight in the 'branch' near our house to insure their ability to make the trip to church the next day. The bed of the carriage had been remade so that it was very long behind the one seat, allowing room for my two brothers, myself, and a small sister to be packed in for our regular trips to church or less frequent ones to town.

"On one occasion an itinerant preacher was holding a protracted meeting at our school house. This meeting occurred almost every fall and often at other seasons of the year. During its continuance, a preaching service was held every night and was attended by nearly everyone in the neighborhood. Some came for the purpose of sincerely worshipping their Maker. Others came for entertainment or out of pure curiosity, but all came.

"As usual, my father was host to the preacher. This meant that he gave the visiting 'brother' free board and lodging, transportation to and from the meeting, free laundry service for both his shirts, and much moral support. This particular guest preacher was a little, round-shouldered, insignificant looking old man who shaved himself recklessly once each week, wore baggy trousers, a blue shirt frayed at collar and cuffs, no tie, and very tousled greying hair. His speech was low and slow and often ungrammatical, but a fervor burned in his watery blue eyes that compelled the respect of an unprejudiced observer. Each night, the schoolroom was filled to overflowing. Something about this meek, uncultured man of God, probably his very evident sincerity, compelled the attendance night after night of these hard-working country folk.

"One night during the course of these meetings, **old Fanny fell seriously ill.**

"Fanny was an essential unit in our lives. Without her that long-bodied carriage could no longer carry us to church, and with only one mule Father could scarcely till his barren little farm. Her death would be a major disaster. My father and the little grey preacher worked for hours over this sick mule. They dosed her with many concoctions. They rubbed her. They covered the trembling animal with old sacks to keep her warm, for the night was cold and the stable draughty. They did everything within their means to save Fanny's life.

"I was too young to be of any assistance, so was spared the pain of leaving my warm blankets on the kitchen floor, where I slept to make room for the visiting preacher in the bed with my two brothers. But I was not too young to feel the gravity of the situation and to thrill to the changes in Fanny's condition as the men returned to the house at intervals to warm themselves, to secure new medicines and supplies, and to consult with each other as to ways and means to cheat death of his victim. I would doze luxuriously and wake to find the two men stamping into the kitchen, beating their hands together to keep up the circulation, or find them huddled over the kitchen stove in earnest conversation.

"All at once I was wide awake. It must have been nearly morning. The kerosene lamp burned low on the oilcloth covered table, as it had done all night, and on their knees, each bowed over a creaky old kitchen chair, were the weary forms of the two men. The voice of the little seedy-looking preacher, solemn, slow, low-pitched, came to my ears. 'O kind God, spare the life of this mule. Restore her to health and strength, for Thou knowest, O Lord, this brother's need for a team. Lord, how can he feed his little ones if Thou takest away this means of support? Thou knowest, kind Lord, we have done our best. In Thy able hands we leave the issue and commit our tired bodies to rest— Amen.' I had a guilty feeling of eavesdropping on this soul as he bared his heart to his God. I fell asleep.

"The next morning, to no one's surprise, apparently **the sick mule was as good as ever.** She ate and drank and pursued her even and unwilling course.

"That night the school house was, if anything, more crowded than usual. Through some chance, I do not know what, a conspicuous stranger was in the congregation. But he was not crowded, though the room was packed. His cold self-sufficiency, high, proud, almost arrogant expression, no less than his clerical suit of deepest black, carefully pressed, silk-lined, set off with snow white linen at neck and wrists, protected him from the too near approach of these humble people. He was looked upon with awe and admiration.

"He did not need to tell us that he was a bishop of the church. He was very clearly one set apart. He was not as other men. His very evident superiority set him above criticism or envy. It was almost presumptuous for us to expect the great bishop to worship the God of our little rural community. But, there he sat; and before his critical eyes must the little, untutored preacher attempt to bring the Gospel message to these young people.

"Young as I was, I sensed rather than knew the embarrassment of the whole roomful of folk, and my heart beat with real fear as the humble old preacher haltingly arose and turned to face the congregation. How could this shabby-looking, unlettered man lift his eyes from the floor in the august presence of the mighty bishop of the church? I think our hearts bled as the little man lifted his eyes to meet the cold stare of the bishop.

"But lift his eyes he did, and he told his simple story of Christ's love for sinners and His sacrifices that all might have eternal life. His words came slowly, almost hesitantly, but so honestly that all as usual forgot the man, his baggy trousers, and his soiled shirt. They remembered only his words. All except the bishop. The bishop's expression remained cold. He made no move, he said no word in response to the spirit of the speaker, until the preacher at the close of his sermon illustrated the power of prayer and the ever presence of God in our daily lives with the story of the sick mule of last night, very evidently saved by the prayers of himself and my father. **The bishop seemed to have reached the limit of his endurance.**

"He did not laugh out loud, but you felt that in his mind he was laughing us all to scorn. He did not ask for a chance to speak, yet he compelled an invitation to dispel such heresy. He rose in his place with great dignity, and in scorching words which I have long ago forgotten he held the pitiable, insignificant, ignorant little itinerant preacher up, and exposed him to the scorn of the world. The idea that the great God of the universe, the God of this holy bishop, could be interested in a mule, was absurd. Almost equally absurd was it that the great Jehovah would hear and answer any prayer of this poorly-equipped, unordained little preacher who stood with bowed head and sagging shoulders during the tirade. The bishop concluded by sarcastically requesting the prayers of a man so close to God that he could cure a mule of a deadly sickness. He declared that he would like to have this powerful supplication on his own behalf. The bishop sat down.

"The little preacher, still standing, bowed yet lower his head, extended his right arm toward Heaven, and there issued from his untrained lips the sweetest, calmest, most poignant prayer it has ever been my lot to hear. 'O kind God, in Thy infinite wisdom and mercy, come down to us and be with this bishop. Make him a tower of strength for Thee. Fill his heart with mercy for the weak and erring ones. Show him daily Thy face of mercy. Fill his veins with the milk of human kindness. Pardon him of his errors of judgment. Lengthen his arm to strive mightily for Thee. Reward him with a peace and contentment in his heart that is not of this earth. God be merciful to me a sinner. Amen.'

"The bishop was on his knees sobbing.

"His huge frame shook with the force of his emotion. Women all over the room were sobbing and praying audibly. Men turned their faces from their neighbors as they surreptitiously wiped their eyes with gnarled knuckles. Once more the minds and hearts of that assembly were centered upon the lowly Jesus and His love for erring man. The very doors of Heaven seemed to open in that dingy schoolroom. Worldly differences of wealth, position, clothes, and education became as nothing. It was as though the little preacher had disappeared, and the great God of the universe, in his place, was pleading for the hearts of His people. Half a dozen Christian men and women nearest the bishop, no longer fearing him, grasped his hands, patted him lovingly on the back, and, with shining faces, welcomed him into the brotherhood of God."

Books on Prayer by E. F. & L Harvey

Kneeling We Triumph, Books 1 & 2
Each book contains 60 stimulating readings composed of gleanings from the writings of godly men and women.

Royal Exchange
31 daily readings on prayer

How They Prayed, Volumes 1, 2, & 3
Volume 1 deals with the subject of household prayer, citing many instances of striking answers that have been received.

Volume 2 reveals how godly ministers of the past have had to spend many hours in prayer in order to see lasting results.

Volume 3 shows how missionaries who have done exploits for God and successfully invaded the kingdom of darkness have prayed hard and long. The book also records the mighty praying that has accompanied past revivals.

Asking Father
A book intended for children but which makes excellent reading for adults also. These short factual stories show the wonderful interest and concern of our Heavenly Father Who delights to hear and answer the prayers of His children.

CPSIA information can be obtained
at www.ICGtesting.com
Printed in the USA
BVOW03s2037041217
501667BV00038B/78/P

9 781932 774764